The Br

POCKET GLOSSARY OF

Literary Terms

compiled by
Laura Buzzard and Don LePan

with contributions from the following:

The Broadview Anthology of Poetry
edited by Herbert Rosengarten and Amanda Goldrick-Jones

The Broadview Anthology of Drama
edited by Jennifer Wise and Craig S. Walker

The Broadview Anthology of Short Fiction
edited by Julia Gaunce, Suzette Mayr, Don LePan,
Marjorie Mather, Bryanne Miller, and Sara Levine

The Broadview Anthology of British Literature
edited by Joseph Black, Leonard Conolly, Kate Flint,
Isobel Grundy, Don LePan, Roy Liuzza, Jerome J. McGann,
Anne Lake Prescott, Barry V. Qualls, and Claire Waters

broadview press

Library and Archives Canada Cataloguing in Publication

Buzzard, Laura, compiler, writer of preface
    The Broadview pocket glossary of literary terms / compiled by Laura Buzzard and Don LePan ; with contributions from the following: the Broadview anthology of poetry edited by Herbert Rosengarten and Amanda Goldrick-Jones, the Broadview anthology of drama edited by Jennifer Wise and Craig S. Walker, the Broadview anthology of short fiction edited by Julia Gaunce, Suzette Mayr, Don LePan, Marjorie Mather, Bryanne Miller, and Sara Levine, the Broadview anthology of British literature edited by Joseph Black, Leonard Conolly, Kate Flint, Isobel Grundy, Don LePan, Roy Liuzza, Jerome J. McGann, Anne Lake Prescott, Barry V. Qualls, Claire Waters.

ISBN 978-1-55481-167-0 (pbk.)

    1. Criticism—Terminology. 2. Literature—Terminology. 3. English language—Terms and phrases. 4. Literary form—Terminology. I. LePan, Don, 1954-, compiler, writer of preface II. Title. III. Title: Glossary of literary terms. IV. Title: Literary terms. V. Title: Pocket glossary of literary terms.

PN44.5.B89 2013   803   C2013-907382-5

Broadview Press is an independent, international publishing house, incorporated in 1985.

We welcome comments and suggestions regarding any aspect of our publications—please feel free to contact us at the addresses below or at broadview@broadviewpress.com.

North America	PO Box 1243, Peterborough, Ontario, Canada K9J 7H5
	2215 Kenmore Ave., Buffalo, New York, USA 14207
	Tel: (705) 743-8990; Fax: (705) 743-8353
	email: customerservice@broadviewpress.com
UK, Europe, Central Asia,	Eurospan Group
Middle East, Africa, India,	3 Henrietta St., London WC2E 8LU, United Kingdom
and Southeast Asia	Tel: 44 (0) 1767 604972; Fax: 44 (0) 1767 601640
	email: eurospan@turpin-distribution.com
Australia and	NewSouth Books c/o TL Distribution
New Zealand	15-23 Helles Ave., Moorebank, NSW, Australia 2170
	Tel: (02) 8778 9999; Fax: (02) 8778 9944
	email: orders@tldistribution.com.au

Edited by Martin Boyne

www.broadviewpress.com

Broadview Press acknowledges the financial support of the Government of Canada through the Canada Book Fund for our publishing activities.

The inside pages of this book are printed on paper containing 100% postconsumer fibre.

PRINTED IN CANADA

The Broadview

POCKET GLOSSARY OF

Literary Terms

◉ PREFACE

The original impetus for this book came out of a realization that putting together the glossaries prepared for a variety of different Broadview anthologies would provide the substance of a very good concise glossary of literary terms—something that would be more portable (and far less expensive) than many of the glossaries currently available. Many of the entries have indeed been drawn from those other Broadview volumes, but as the book has taken shape we have found ourselves going considerably beyond the material found in them. In particular, we have added a number of longer entries on larger or more complex topics. Along the way, we have been somewhat surprised to discover quite a few terms that seem to us to be of significance to literary studies but that are not often included in other glossaries; such topics we have also added here. We have made it a practice not to write separate entries on individual authors, literary theorists, etc., but have provided brief notes directing readers to the topic entries in which those individuals are discussed, quoted, or otherwise mentioned.

Here and there, we have included some information that might be deemed inessential but that seems to us to be of real potential interest to those who already have a substantial background in English studies. For the most part, though, we have aimed the book at an undergraduate audience. With this in mind, we have tried to keep the book concise—both in the selection of terms and in the definitions themselves—and, whenever possible, to incorporate helpful illustrative examples. Our hope is that this little volume will make a wide range of sometimes difficult topics more readily understandable to the student and to the general reader.

*   *   *

In addition to those listed on the title page who made contributions, we would like to thank Martin Boyne (of Trent University), Jessica De Villiers (of the University of British Columbia), Adam Frank (of the University of British Columbia), Maureen Okun (of Vancouver Island University), and Nicole Shukin (of the University of Victoria)—all of whom offered helpful advice regarding particular entries.

Don LePan and Laura Buzzard

◎ GLOSSARY

Abel, Lionel: see *metatheater*.

Abrams, M.H.: see *dramatic monologue / persona poem / dramatic poem*.

absurdist: characterized by a minimalist style and bleak worldview. The term is most frequently used with reference to certain plays of the post-World War II period (notable examples include Samuel Beckett's *Waiting for Godot* and Tom Stoppard's *Rosencrantz and Guildenstern Are Dead*). Such works seem set in a world stripped of faith in God or a rational cosmos, in which idealism has been lost, and human action and communication are futile. Absurdist characters are often portrayed as trapped in a pointless round of trivial, self-defeating acts of comical repetitiveness. For this reason, absurdism can verge on *farce* or *black comedy*. See also *existentialism*.

accent: in poetry, the natural emphasis (stress) that speakers place on a syllable.

accentual-syllabic verse: poetry in which a line is measured by the number of syllables and by the pattern of accented (stressed) and unaccented (unstressed) syllables. This is the most common metrical system in English verse.

accentual verse: poetry in which a line is measured only by the number of accents or stresses, not by the number of syllables.

acephalous line: see *headless line*.

a

acts [of a play]: the sections into which a play or other theatrical work have been divided, either by the playwright or by a later editor. During the *Renaissance*, it became popular to divide plays into five acts in imitation of Roman practice; modern works are sometimes divided into three.

Adams, Carol J.: see *animal studies*.

Aesthetes: members of a late-nineteenth-century movement that valued "art for art's sake"—for its purely aesthetic qualities—as opposed to valuing art for the moral content it may convey, for the intellectual stimulation it may provide, or for a range of other qualities.

affect: a term that English studies has borrowed from psychology and then adapted in a number of ways. At its most basic, "affect" refers to the ways in which humans are affected by outside stimuli—especially stimuli that relate to what have traditionally been referred to as the emotions. Affect studies and affect theory are now established sub-disciplines in literary studies and have developed a wide range of approaches to, and interpretations of, affect, covering such areas as aesthetics, ethics, and political economy, to name only a few.

Of the several distinct strains of affect theory, perhaps the most influential has been the one deriving from the work of psychologist Silvan Tomkins (1911-91), who argued that affects are distinct from human emotions, and that, whereas emotions are complex and often overlap with one another, affects fall into discrete categories, usually occurring in pairs (among them anger-rage, distress-anguish, fear-terror, enjoyment-joy, interest-excitement, shame-humiliation, and surprise-startle). According to Tomkins, all affects are rooted in biology. Though affects may correspond to what humans term "emotions" in non-human animals, Tomkins theorizes that quite different mechanisms operate in humans. To pick one example, he suggests that both intellectual curiosity and sexual lust have, in humans, the affect of interest-excitement at their core; this affect is then combined in quite different ways with various drives, perceptions, and objects to produce two very different emotions.

Another strain of affect studies rejects Tomkins's categories and does not see a clear dividing line between affect and emotion; scholars in this group often work in empiricist traditions with roots in the nineteenth-century work of Charles Darwin (1809-82), in which human emotions are seen as extensions (albeit more complex ones) of those that we may find in non-human animals.

A third, quite different, strain of affect theory draws on the work of French theorist Gilles Deleuze (1925-95), who (largely through his reading of the seventeenth-century philosopher Baruch Spinoza's *Ethics*) drew connections between human emotional and moral feelings and endeavored to understand them collectively in the context of socio-economic forces (in particular, those of capitalism).

Among the best known of the numerous literary theorists who have done important work in the field are Lauren Berlant (b. 1957), whose books have done much to encourage a wide-ranging re-assessment of the literature of sentiment, and Eve Kosofsky Sedgwick (1950-2009), whose wide-ranging body of work includes explorations of the connections between feeling (and the performance of feeling) and political action.

agitprop: political *propaganda*, particularly that which takes the form of literature, art, or theater. The term derives from a Russian phrase meaning "agitation and propaganda" and, in the twentieth century, was applied specifically to communist propaganda sponsored by the Soviet government. In English, "agitprop" has a negative connotation and can be applied to use of the arts for propaganda of any sort.

alexandrine: a line of verse that is twelve syllables long. In English verse, the alexandrine is always an *iambic hexameter*: that is, it has six iambic *feet*. The most often quoted example is the second line in a couplet from Alexander Pope's *Essay on Criticism* (1711): "A needless Alexandrine ends the song / That, like a wounded snake, drags its slow length along." See also *Spenserian stanza*.

alienation effect: a Russian concept, also known by the German term *Verfremdungseffekt*, popularized by Bertolt Brecht (1898-1956); it refers to any technique used in the theatre to distance spectators from the performance to the point where they can view it critically and ask questions about it. To alienate a phenomenon is to "make it strange," to make it seem odd or surprising. Actors do this when they keep their character at a distance rather than merging with it, or deliver their lines as if in quotation marks; directors use the "A-effect" when they interrupt the action or call attention to its artificiality with music, slides, or lighting. The opposite of "to alienate" is "to naturalize."

allegory: a narrative with both a literal meaning and secondary, often symbolic meaning or meanings. Allegory frequently employs *personification* to give concrete embodiment to abstract concepts or entities, such as feelings or personal qualities. It may also present one set of characters or events in the guise of another, using implied parallels for the purposes of *satire* or political comment, as in John Dryden's poem "Absalom and Achitophel" (1681-82).

Allen, Grant: see *New Woman literature*.

alliteration: the grouping of words with the same initial consonant (e.g., "break, blow, burn, and make me new"). The repetition of sound acts as a connector. See also *assonance* and *consonance*.

alliterative verse: poetry that employs alliteration of stressed syllables in each line as its chief structural principle. Alliterative verse is the dominant poetic form in Old English poetry, each line of which typically features two half lines, each with two stressed syllables; in most cases the stressed syllables alliterate. The alliterative revival of the fourteenth century brought the tradition of alliterative verse back into the mainstream of literary culture in Britain; *Sir Gawain and the Green Knight* and *Piers Plowman* are among the best known of fourteenth-century alliterative poems in English. A couple of lines from *Sir Gawain* may give the flavor:

> Then the gome in the grene graythed hym swythe,
> Gederez up hys grymme tole Gawayn to smyte;

allusion: a reference, often indirect or unidentified, to a person, thing, or event. A reference in one literary work to another literary work, whether to its content or its form, also constitutes an allusion. See also *intertextuality*.

ambiguity: an "opening" of language created by the writer to allow for multiple meanings or differing interpretations. In literature, ambiguity may be deliberately employed by the writer to enrich meaning; this differs from any unintentional, unwanted, ambiguity in non-literary prose.

amphibrach: a metrical *foot* of three syllables, with a stressed syllable between two unstressed ones, x / x (e.g., "sensation").

amphigory: verse consisting of words that have been combined to make pleasing sounds but little sense.

anachronism: accidental or intentional attribution of people, things, ideas, or events to historical periods in which they do not and could not possibly belong.

anadiplosis: repetition of the last word or phrase of one sentence or line of poetry at the beginning of the next (e.g., "The children stopped by the sea. / The sea was filled with ships, / The ships were filled with guns, / The guns had mouths with lips, / The lips were filled with hate").

anagram: word or phrase constructed of the transposed letters of another word or phrase. The title of Samuel Butler's *Erewhon* (1872) is an anagram of "nowhere."

analepsis: see *flashback*.

analogy: a broad term that refers to our processes of noting similarities among things or events. Specific forms of analogy in poetry include *simile* and *metaphor*.

anapest: a metrical *foot* containing two unstressed syllables followed by one stressed syllable: x x / (e.g., "underneath," "intervene").

anaphora: a classical rhetorical device in which the same word or words are used to begin a series of two or more poetic lines, sentences, or phrases. In this example from Matthew Arnold's "Dover Beach" (1867), the repetitions of "so" and "nor" are both instances of anaphora: "... the world, which seems / To lie before us like a land of dreams, / So various, so beautiful, so new, / Hath really neither joy, nor love, nor light, / Nor certitude, nor peace, nor help for pain...."

animal studies: an umbrella term for a broad range of academic inquiries into matters relating to non-human animals—including by philosophers, historians, biologists, anthropologists, and legal scholars, as well as literary critics and theorists. The most visible landmarks in modern-day animal studies are works by philosophers—chief among them Peter Singer's *Animal Liberation* (1975), which made a range of powerful arguments on specific topics (most notably, the cruelties of modern-day factory farming), and argued more broadly that humans unreasonably discriminate against other species. Other philosophers who have made influential contributions to the debate over the status of non-human animals include Tom Regan (b. 1938), who has made a comprehensive case that many non-human animals should be considered to have rights; Mary Midgley (b. 1919), who has made the case for considering many non-human animals to be persons; and Gary Francione (b. 1954), the most influential proponent of the view that non-human animals must be treated as independent entities legally, rather than as commodities.

These writers, all of whom work in the analytic tradition of philosophy, have had a powerful influence on activists and on public policy. But continental philosophers—Jacques Derrida (1930-2004) most notable among them—have exerted a stronger influence than have analytic philosophers on animal studies as it has taken shape as a branch of literary theory. Derrida's arguments and linguistic practice have been varied and inventive. From the title of "The Animal that Therefore I Am (more to follow)" (2002; original French title "L'Animal qui donc je suis [à suivre]"), one might think that the author would emphasize the animality that humans have in common with other animals. Instead, though he certainly acknowledges that element, Derrida places at least as much emphasis on the otherness to humans of non-human animals, even their "absolute alterity." He argues that "the property unique to animals and what in the final analysis distinguishes them from man, is their being naked without knowing it"; and he makes clear his opposition to the creation of "a single large set, a single, great, fundamentally homogenous and continuous family tree" that includes both homo sapiens and other animals. Yet he is also at pains to acknowledge what he calls "the animal in me." Derrida's arguments often seem to run in more than one direction simultaneously—and his work has stimulated work by scholars in English studies in more than one direction as well.

a

In the early years of the twenty-first century, animal studies has made itself a presence within literary studies largely through theoretical work done by those who describe their field as *critical* animal studies, of whom Cary Wolfe is the most prominent figure. Critical animal studies aims to connect the ways in which humans have interacted with non-human animals with broader social and economic forces, and with the ways in which knowledge is constructed in human societies—Western societies in particular. Wolfe and others have suggested strong parallels between the oppression by humans of non-human animals and other forms of oppression—and have suggested too that questions of how to reduce such oppression should be seen not in isolation but as part of a larger project of reshaping the ways in we approach the world as a whole. More specifically, Wolfe has argued against the rights-based discourse of humanism and called for a post-humanist approach to expanding the moral community. With such an approach, we would value non-human animals not because they are necessarily similar to humans, but in conjunction with an acknowledgment of their difference.

Other important figures in animal studies as it connects to literary studies include Carol J. Adams (b. 1951), who has done much to show how feminism may connect with animal studies, and Donna Haraway, whose *Primate Visions* (1990) and *When Species Meet* (2007) have helped to frame animal studies in cultural and interdisciplinary terms.

The growth in interest among theorists in questions relating to human and non-human animals has been paralleled by a growth in interest in these questions among writers of fiction; important late-twentieth- and early-twenty-first-century works in this area include J.M. Coetzee's *The Lives of Animals* (1997) and the larger work into which it was incorporated, the novel *Elizabeth Costello* (2003); Barbara Gowdy's novel *The White Bone*

(1999), written from the point of view of its elephant characters; Ruth Ozeki's satirical novel about the meat industry, *My Year of Meats* (1998); and a non-fiction work by the novelist Jonathan Safran Foer, *Eating Animals* (2009), which marshals arguments against consuming the products of factory farming while also providing a memoir of the author's experiences as he gave up eating animals.

The past decade has also seen a substantial increase in interest among literary scholars in analyzing works from other eras that are in one way or another concerned with non-human animals— from Anna Sewell's *Black Beauty* (1877) and Jack London's *The Call of the Wild* (1903) to H.G. Wells's novel about experimentation on non-human animals, *The Island of Dr. Moreau* (1896).

annotations: notes to a text; they may take the form of footnotes, endnotes, or marginal glosses.

Anouilh, Jean: see *chorus*.

antagonist: in a literary work, a major character or group of characters in conflict with the *protagonist*. Although protagonists are often morally good and antagonists morally bad, this is not always the case.

anticlimax: a plot development or an arrangement of material that leaves readers or audience feeling that what has been presented is less dramatic or important than they have been led to expect. The following example is from Alexander Pope's *Rape of the Lock* (1712): "Not youthful kings in battle seized alive, / Not scornful virgins who their charms survive, / Not ardent lovers robbed of all their bliss, / Not ancient ladies when refused a kiss, / Nor tyrants fierce that unrepenting die, / Not Cynthia when her manteau's pinned awry, / E'er felt such rage, resentment, and despair, / As thou, sad virgin! for thy ravished hair."

antihero: leading character possessing traits largely or entirely unlike those traditionally associated with heroism.

antimasque: see *masque*.

antistrophe: from Greek drama: the chorus's countermovement or reply to an initial movement (*strophe*). See *ode*.

antithesis: an opposite. More specifically, the term is applied to a rhetorical device in which opposing concepts are placed close together, with *parallel* phrasing, in order to emphasize their difference. The device was especially popular among eighteenth-century poets such as Alexander Pope; the following example is from Pope's *Rape of the Lock* (1712-17): "Charms strike the sight, but merit wins the soul."

aphorism: a brief saying, typically purporting to offer a general truth. "Life is short, art is long" is the best known of the *Aphorisms* of the fifth-/fourth-century BCE Greek writer Hippocrates.

apocalyptic literature: literature dealing with catastrophic events or their aftermath, often with a strong suggestion that the destruction of the entire world may be imminent.

apocryphal: in everyday usage, "apocryphal" means "of dubious or uncertain origin." Abraham Lincoln's supposed remark to Harriet Beecher Stowe, "So you're the little woman who wrote the book that made this great war," is apocryphal in this sense; there is no firm evidence that Lincoln said any such thing.

In one core literary meaning, "apocryphal" refers to those books of the Bible that are not accepted by some Christians as being part of the sacred canon. By extension, the word has also come to be used to refer to a work that has been attributed in whole or in part to a particular author, but that is not universally accepted as part of that author's canon of work. Plays such as *Sir*

Thomas More and *The Two Noble Kinsmen*, for example (both of which Shakespeare probably wrote some part of, but neither of which is accepted as being entirely by Shakespeare), are referred to as part of the Shakespeare Apocrypha.

a

Apollonian: associated with reasoned thought, formally ordered works of art, and moral clarity. The German philosopher Friedrich Nietzsche (1844-1900) coined the term (after Apollo, the Greek god of light), and contrasted the Apollonian with the Dionysian (after Dionysus, the Greek god of wine and revelry), associating the latter with the wildly irrational, the disordered, and the ecstatic.

apology: in its literary sense, an "apology" for something is a defense of that thing; in his *Apology for Poetry* (1579-80), for example, Sir Philip Sidney is not saying he is sorry.

aporia: difficulty that is impossible to resolve. In the vocabulary of ancient Greek and Roman *rhetoric*, the nature of such difficulty may be entirely rhetorical; a politician who professes to be unable to decide whether the duplicity or the incompetence of her opponent is more disturbing is using aporia as a rhetorical device. Jacques Derrida (1930-2004) and others have used the term to refer to very real points of difficulty in which texts undermine their own apparent meaning, leaving us with a double bind in which it is impossible to decide between incompatible meanings.

apostrophe: in its literary sense, a *figure of speech* (a *trope*) in which a writer directly addresses an object—or a dead or absent person—as if the imagined audience were actually listening.

apposition: A word or phrase placed in apposition to another word or phrase follows it immediately and has the same grammatical structure (e.g., "Carol Ann Duffy, Britain's Poet Laureate, will be delivering the Gustafson lecture in Nanaimo this week").

apron: the part of a stage that extends into the auditorium or audience beyond the *proscenium* arch; sometimes called a forestage or a thrust stage.

archaism: the use, for literary effect, of old-fashioned or obsolete words or phrasings.

Archer, William: see *narratology / narrative theory*.

archetype: in literature and mythology, a recurring idea, *symbol*, *motif*, character, or place. To some scholars and psychologists, an archetype represents universal human thought-patterns or experiences. See *mythopoeic theory and criticism*.

arena theater: see *theater-in-the-round*.

Aristophanes: see *Hellenic / Hellenistic*.

Aristotle: see *anagnorisis, catharsis, ethos, hamartia, Hellenic / Hellenistic, humanism / Renaissance humanism, logos, mimesis, narratology / narrative theory, peripeteia, plot, poetics, Theory, unities*.

Armantrout, Rae: see *language poetry*.

Arnold, Matthew: see *anaphora*.

art for art's sake: see *Aesthetes*.

artificial: often used as a term of praise in the sixteenth and seventeenth centuries: a well-constructed literary work could be described as "wonderfully artificial," with reference to the artifice displayed by its maker. In the eighteenth century critics began to place the artificial in opposition to the natural, and to disparage the former as being too obviously contrived.

Ascham, Roger: see *humanism / Renaissance humanism*.

aside: words delivered by actors to the audience, or by characters to themselves, which by *convention* are treated as if they were inaudible to the other characters on stage.

assonance: the repetition of identical or similar vowel sounds in stressed syllables in which the surrounding consonants are different: for example, "shame" and "fate"; "gale" and "cage"; or the long "i" sounds in "Beside the pumice isle...."

asyndeton: a form of *ellipsis* in which conjunctions are omitted for rhetorical or literary purposes, despite being required for the sentence to be completely grammatically correct. In the following example from a sixteenth-century song by John Dowland, the omission of "and" after the word "faint" is an example of asyndeton: "I sit, I sigh, I weep, I faint, I die / In deadly pain and endless misery."

atmosphere: see *tone*.

Atwood, Margaret: see *mythopoeic theory and criticism, speculative fiction*.

aubade: a lyric poem that greets or laments the arrival of dawn.

Auerbach, Erich: see *Theory*.

Augusta, Lady Gregory: see *Irish Literary Renaissance*.

Austen, Jane: see *free indirect style / free indirect discourse, juvenilia, sentiment*.

author: an individual who creates an artistic work. The concept of authorship has long been recognized as problematic with regard to works such as *The Odyssey*, *The Iliad*, or *Beowulf*, where texts are presumed to have deep roots in oral tradition; and also with regard to unattributed works such as medieval *biblical plays*, where authorship may well have been collaborative and texts

a

may have evolved over decades, or in some cases even centuries. In the 1960s the concept of authorship was called into question more generally in two influential essays, Roland Barthes's "The Death of the Author" (1968) and Michel Foucault's "What is an Author?" (1969). Barthes decried the "invention" of the author; he saw no reason to limit the meanings readers gleaned from texts on the basis of any presumption as to what an author may have intended the text to mean. Foucault saw the concept of authorship as anachronistic and inappropriately individualistic; according to his view, a text could better be understood as a cultural construct than as the product of a single mind.

autobiography: see *life writing*.

avant-garde: in military terminology, the advance guard that leads the way; in cultural terminology, the group(s) who are continually aiming to "make it new" (in Ezra Pound's phrase)—to develop artistic forms that challenge established artistic traditions.

Bach, Johann Sebastian: see *baroque*.

Bacon, Francis: see *expressionism / impressionism*.

ballad: a folk song or poem that tells a dramatic story, often one based on legend or history. A distinction is usually drawn between folk or traditional ballads, which were intended to be sung and were transmitted through an oral tradition, and literary ballads, which were written for the page by individual authors who adopted the style of traditional ballads. Folk ballads have been written since the Middle Ages; literary ballads became common in the eighteenth century.

ballade: a *fixed form* most commonly characterized by only three rhymes, with an eight-line stanza rhyming *ababbcbc* and an *envoy* rhyming *bcbc*. Both Geoffrey Chaucer (1343-1400) and

Dante Gabriel Rossetti (e.g., "Ballad of the Dead Ladies," 1869) adopted this form.

ballad stanza: a *quatrain* with alternating four-stress and three-stress lines, rhyming *abcb*. A variant is "common measure," in which the alternating lines are strictly *iambic* and rhyme *abab*.

Balzac, Honoré de: see *semiotics*.

baroque: powerful and substantially ornamented in style, often characterized by striking contrasts and by a strong (but not sensationalized) sense of the dramatic. As a term in the history of visual art and of music, "Baroque" is usually capitalized and is much more precise in meaning, referring to the work of such early-seventeenth-century figures as Rembrandt (in painting) and J.S. Bach (in music). The late Baroque forms that prevailed from the late seventeenth century until well into the eighteenth tended toward fewer dramatic contrasts, more ornamentation, and rather less seriousness; such styles are often termed "Rococo." As literary critical terms, "baroque" and "rococo" may both be used to describe work in these styles of any era.

Barthes, Roland: see *author, binary thinking, intentional fallacy, semiotics, structuralism / poststructuralism*.

Bashō / Matsuo Bashō: see *haiku*.

bathos: an anticlimactic effect brought about by a writer's descent from an elevated subject or tone to the ordinary or trivial.

Beardsley, Monroe: see *intentional fallacy, New Criticism*.

Beat Writing: The "Beats" were American writers of the 1950s and 1960s, centered largely in San Francisco, who promoted a rebellious and anti-establishment view of the world, made famous through Jack Kerouac's novel *On the Road* (1957) and reflected in experimental works such as William Burroughs's novel *The Naked Lunch* (1959) and Allen Ginsberg's poem *Howl* (1956).

Bechdel, Alison: see *graphic literature*.

Beckett, Samuel: see *absurdist, Irish Literary Renaissance, monodrama*.

Behn, Aphra: see *comedy of manners, novel, Restoration comedy*.

***belles lettres*:** writing valued primarily for its aesthetic qualities, rather than for the meanings it communicates to the reader. Scientific or philosophical writing, for example, falls outside of the category of *belles lettres*.

Benjamin, Walter: see *Marxist theory and criticism*.

Bentley, Edmund Clerihew: see *Clerihew*.

Berlant, Lauren: see *affect*.

Bernstein, Charles: see *language poetry*.

biblical plays: a term now commonly used to refer to plays on biblical themes that were performed beginning in the late fourteenth century in several English towns, often in conjunction with festival days of late spring or summer (notably Whitsun, Pentecost, and the Feast of Corpus Christi). Such plays continued to be performed until their suppression in the late sixteenth century. In the case of the northern towns of York and Chester (but only in those two instances), such plays survive in more-or-less unified sequences (often called pageants) that present the full sweep of biblical history.

Several terms previously used to name this sort of drama (including "miracle plays," "mystery plays," and "cycle plays") are now considered to be in one way or another problematic as blanket terms.

Bildungsroman: a novel tracing the psychological, moral, or spiritual development of a young person.

binary thinking: the tendency to categorize objects or concepts into oppositional sets of two. Twentieth-century *structuralist* and *poststructuralist* thinkers, notably Claude Lévi-Strauss (1908-2009) and Roland Barthes (1915-80), drew attention to this human tendency, suggesting that it carried with it a tendency to oversimplify and to distort—and suggesting too that binaries that humans may imagine to involve two fixed characteristics (e.g., wild / tame; masculine / feminine; beautiful / ugly) do not in fact capture any fixed entities; rather they give expression in words to fluid relationships that are defined more than anything by our underlying assumptions.

b

biography: see *life writing*.

black comedy: humor based on death, horror, or any incongruously macabre subject matter.

Black Mountain School: a group of American writers, including Robert Creeley (1926-2005) and Charles Olson (1910-70), associated with Black Mountain College in North Carolina in the 1940s and 1950s. Their work is associated with experimentalism and a rejection of conventional forms in literature and the creative arts.

Blake, William: see *symbol*.

blank verse: unrhymed lines written in *iambic pentameter*. (The form was introduced to English verse by Henry Howard, Earl of Surrey, in his 1547 translation of parts of Virgil's *Aeneid*.)

blend: see *portmanteau word*.

bob-and-wheel: a set of rhymed lines appearing at the end of a section of non-rhyming *alliterative verse*, typically beginning with a very short line (the "bob") that is rhymed with two of the following four longer lines (the "wheel"). Below is an example (in modernized spelling) from the fourteenth-century poem *Sir Gawain and the Green Knight*; the line "Nay none evil ... wysten" is the last of 18 non-rhyming alliterative lines in the stanza; "But bliss" is the bob; and the following four rhyming lines make up the "wheel":

> Nay none evil on neither halve, neither they wysten
> > But bliss.
> > They laughed and layked long;
> > At the last she can him kiss
> > Her leave fair can she fong,
> > And went her way, iwisse.

Boccaccio, Giovanni: see *novel*.

bombast: inappropriately inflated or grandiose language.

Borges, Jorge Luis: see *magic realism*.

bowdlerize: Thomas Bowdler's *The Family Shakespeare* (the first edition of which appeared in 1807) aimed to sanitize Shakespeare's language so as "to present to the public an edition of his plays which the parent, the guardian, or the instructor of youth may place without fear in the hands of the pupil." A debate in 1812 in two literary journals as to the merits of the endeavor sparked sales, making the work a sudden bestseller, and bringing "bowdlerize" into common currency as a term for expurgating literary works so as to make their language and content more respectable.

Braddon, Mary Elizabeth: see *sensation literature*.

Brecht, Bertolt: see *alienation effect, Marxist theory and criticism*.

broken rhyme: rhyme in which a multi-syllable word is split at the end of a line and continued onto the next, to allow an end-rhyme with the split syllable.

Brontë, Charlotte: see *feminism / feminist criticism and theory / gender-based criticism and theory*.

Brooks, Cleanth: see *close readings, New Criticism*.

Browning, Elizabeth Barrett: see *novel*.

Browning, Robert: see *dramatic monologue / persona poem / dramatic poem*.

burlesque: *satire* of an especially exaggerated sort, particularly one that ridicules its subject by emphasizing its vulgar or ridiculous aspects.

Burney, Frances: see *epistolary novel*.

Burroughs, William: see *Beat Writing*.

Buruma, Ian: see *Orientalism*.

Butler, Judith: see *feminism / feminist criticism and theory / gender-based criticism and theory, queer theory*.

Butler, Samuel: see *anagram*.

Byron, Lord George Gordon: see *ottava rima*.

cacophony: a harsh, displeasing combination of sounds, in contrast to *euphony*.

caesura: an internal pause in a line of verse.

Cain, James: see *noir*.

Calvin, John: see *humanism / Renaissance humanism*.

Campion, Thomas: see *quantity*, *symbol*.

canon: in literature, those works that are commonly accepted as possessing authority or importance. In practice, "canonical" texts or authors are those that are discussed most frequently by scholars and taught most frequently in university courses.

canto: a sub-section of a long (usually epic) poem.

canzone: a short song or poem, with stanzas of equal length and an *envoy*.

caricature: an exaggerated and simplified depiction of character; the reduction of a personality to one or two telling traits at the expense of all other nuances and contradictions.

***carpe diem*:** Latin (from Horace) meaning "seize the day." The idea of enjoying the moment is a common one in *Renaissance* love poetry, as in, for example, Andrew Marvell's mid-seventeenth-century poem "To His Coy Mistress."

Carroll, Lewis: see *nonsense verse*.

catachresis: umbrella term referring to the use of an inappropriate word (such as "conflate" instead of "confound") and to a variety of *figures of speech* (*tropes*) that involve the misuse of words. "Catachresis" can, for example, refer to the appropriation of a technically incorrect word to describe something for which the correct vocabulary does not exist, such as the terms "file folder" and "desktop" when used in the context of a computer. As in those examples, such catachrestic terms frequently become part of everyday language. "Catachresis" also refers to the use of a jarring or self-contradictory figure of speech, either as an instance of bad writing or as a deliberate poetic or rhetorical device; a well-known example of the latter is the phrase "Blind mouths!" in Milton's *Lycidas* (1637).

catalexis: the omission of unstressed syllables from a line of verse (such a line is referred to as "catalectic"). In *iambic* verse it is usually the first syllable of the line that is omitted; in *trochaic*, the last. For example, in the first stanza of A.E. Housman's "To an Athlete Dying Young" (1896), the third line is catalectic: i.e., it omits the first, unstressed syllable called for by the poem's iambic tetrameter form: "The time you won your town the race / We chaired you through the market-place; / Man and boy stood cheering by, / And home we brought you shoulder-high."

catharsis: the arousal through the performance of a dramatic tragedy of "emotions of pity and fear" to a point where "purgation" or "purification" occurs and the feelings are released or transformed. The concept was developed by Aristotle in his *Poetics* (fourth century BCE) from an ancient Greek medical concept, and adapted by him into an aesthetic principle.

Chandler, Raymond: see *noir*.

chanson de geste: French epic poem (or, literally, "song of heroic deeds") of the eleventh to thirteenth centuries, intended to be sung to musical accompaniment. *Chansons de geste* often combine history with legend, and many are incorporated into cycles centered on a particular figure, event, or theme; for example, the best-known *chanson*, the *Chanson de Roland* (c. 1100), is part of a cycle centered on the exploits of Charlemagne. The *chansons de geste* were a source of influence and inspiration for medieval *romances*.

C

chapbook: a very short book with a small trim size (i.e., small page dimensions). In the eighteenth century, pamphlet-size volumes (usually recounting tales of the strange or miraculous) were sold by "chapmen" or peddlers. Now the term is usually applied to short, privately printed books of poetry.

characterization: the means by which an author develops and presents a character's personality qualities and distinguishing traits. A character may be established in the story by descriptive commentary or may be developed less directly—for example, through his or her words, actions, thoughts, and interactions with other characters.

Chaucer, Geoffrey: see *ballade, exemplum, frame narrative, rhyme royal.*

Chaucerian stanza: see *rhyme royal.*

chiasmus: inverted parallelism in writing or speech; chiasmus is a *figure of speech* that reverses the order of words or phrases in successive parallel clauses (e.g., "She gave him love, laughter, and happiness, and happiness, laughter and love were what he gave her in return"; "The ship will be here in the evening; in the morning it will leave").

choliambus: the substitution of a *trochee* or *dactyl* for the final *iamb* in a line of iambic verse (e.g., the trochee "bro-ken" following four iambs in the line, "Away he flung that heavy sword, broken." Like a "soft landing" (or *feminine ending*), a choliambus results in an iambic line ending in an unstressed syllable.

Chopin, Kate: see *imagery.*

choriambus: a poetic *foot* formed of two stressed syllables enclosing two unstressed syllables (/ x x /); rhythmically, a choriambus is equivalent to a *trochee* followed by an *iamb.*

chorus: originally, the choir of singing, dancing, masked young men who performed in ancient Greek *tragedy* and *comedy*. It gradually disappeared from tragedy and comedy, but many attempts have been made to revive some version of it, notably during the Italian and English *Renaissance*, under Weimar Classicism, and by such twentieth-century playwrights as Jean Anouilh (1910-87), T.S. Eliot (1888-1965), and Michel Tremblay (b. 1942).

chronology: the way a story is organized in terms of time. Linear narratives run continuously from one point in time to a later point, while non-linear narratives are non-continuous and may jump forward and backward in time. A *flashback*, in which a story jumps to a scene previous in time, is an example of non-linearity.

Churchill, Caryl: see *expressionism / impressionism*.

Cixous, Hélène: see *feminism / feminist criticism and theory / gender-based criticism and theory, psychoanalytic theory*.

classical: originating in or relating to ancient Greek or Roman culture. As commonly conceived, "classical" implies a strong sense of formal order. The term *neoclassical* is often used with reference to literature of the Restoration and eighteenth century that was strongly influenced by ancient Greek and Roman models.

clerihew: a poetic form created by Edmund Clerihew Bentley (1875-1956). A clerihew is a poem of four lines, rhymed *aabb*, with no regular pattern of rhythm (though the second line is typically considerably longer than the other lines, and the last line usually very short), and with a person as its topic. The person's name forms the first line. Here is an example:

Charles Dickens
Knew how to bring a tangled tale to an end when the
    plot thickens:
The hero, so that loose ends of story could be tied,
Died.

climax: see *Freytag's pyramid*.

closed couplet: a pair of rhyming lines that form a complete unit of thought and are grammatically complete.

close reading: a reading of a literary text that pays close attention to meaning and form on a line-by-line or sentence-by-sentence basis. The approach has close connections to the method of teaching literature in France known as *explication de texte*. In the view of Cleanth Brooks (1906-94) and other *formalist* literary critics of the mid-twentieth century who gave the term "close reading" common currency, literary criticism should be "concerned primarily with the work itself" rather than, for example, with the biographical, historical, or literary context out of which it emerged. As practiced by such critics, close reading tended to focus on *syntax* and on *metaphor* (or other forms of figurative language); the interpretative emphasis tended to be on drawing out ambiguities or paradoxes. Close reading may just as easily focus, however, on entirely different elements—effects of sound in successive lines of poetry, for example, or shifts in *narrative perspective* in successive sentences in a work of prose fiction. And there is no inherent reason why close reading need ignore historical or literary context; the richest close readings often take full account of such things.

closet drama: a play (typically in verse) written for private performance. The term came into use in the first half of the nineteenth century.

closure: the sense of completion evoked at the end of a story when all or most aspects of the major conflicts have been resolved. An example of the resolution of an internal conflict in Charlotte Perkins Gilman's story "The Yellow Wallpaper" (1892) is the narrator's "merging" with the woman behind the paper with which she has been fascinated. Not every narrative has a strong sense of closure.

Coetzee, J.M.: see *animal studies*.

Coleridge, Samuel Taylor: see *marginalia*.

Collins, Wilkie: see *sensation literature*.

colloquial language: everyday or informal language, as opposed to technical, overtly literary, or formal language.

comedy: as a literary term, used originally to denote that class of ancient Greek drama in which the action ends happily. More broadly, the term has been used to describe a wide variety of literary forms of a more or less light-hearted or humorous character.

comedy of manners: a type of comic play that flourished in the late seventeenth century in London, and elsewhere since, which bases its humor on the sexual and marital intrigues of "high society." It is sometimes contrasted with "comedy of character," as its *satire* is directed at the social habits and conventional hypocrisy of the whole leisured class. Also called *Restoration comedy*; exemplified by the plays of Aphra Behn (1640-89), William Wycherley (1641-1715), and William Congreve (1670-1729).

commedia dell'arte: a form of largely improvised comic performance conducted by masked performers and involving considerable physical activity. The genre of *commedia dell'arte* originated in Italy in the sixteenth century; it was influential throughout Europe for more than two centuries thereafter.

common meter: meter in which lines of *iambic tetrameter* alternate with lines of iambic *trimeter*, generally in four-lined stanzas rhymed either *abab* or *abcb*.

Comte, Auguste: see *historicism / new historicism*.

conceit: an unusually elaborate *metaphor* or *simile* that extends beyond its original tenor and vehicle, sometimes becoming a "master" analogy for the entire poem (see, for example, John Donne's "The Flea" and Robert Frost's sonnet "The Silken Tent"). Ingenious or fanciful images and comparisons were especially popular with the *metaphysical poets* of the seventeenth century, giving rise to the term "metaphysical conceit." See also *epic simile*.

concrete poetry: an experimental form, most popular during the 1950s and 1960s, in which the text itself forms a visual image of the poem's key words or ideas. See also *pattern poetry*.

confessional poetry: poetry that presents autobiographical details—especially those regarding taboo topics such as sexuality, mental illness, family conflict, and the body—and is typically written in the first person. The confessional poetry movement flourished in 1950s and 1960s America; poets associated with it include Sylvia Plath (1932-63), Robert Lowell (1917-77), and Anne Sexton (1928-74). Although its popularity waned in the 1970s and 1980s, it has nonetheless exerted a strong influence on late-twentieth- and twenty-first-century poetry.

conflict: struggle between characters and/or between opposing forces. Conflict can be internal (psychological) or external (conflict with another character, for instance, or with society or nature).

Congreve, William: see *comedy of manners*, *Restoration comedy*.

connotation: the implied, often unspoken meaning(s) of a given word, as distinct from its denotation, or literal meaning. Connotations may have highly emotional undertones and are usually culturally specific.

Conrad, Joseph: see *delayed decoding, doppelgänger, expressionism / impressionism, frame narrative.*

consonance: the pairing of words with similar initial and ending consonants, but with different vowel sounds (live/love, wander/wonder). See also *alliteration.*

convention: aesthetic approach, technique, or practice accepted as characteristic and appropriate for a particular form. It is a convention of certain sorts of plays, for example, that the characters speak in blank verse, of other sorts of plays that characters speak in rhymed couplets, and of still other sorts of dramatic performances that characters frequently break into song to express their feelings.

couplet: a pair of rhyming lines, usually in the same meter. If they form a complete unit of thought and are grammatically complete, the lines are known as a *closed couplet.* See also *heroic couplet.*

Cowley, Abraham: see *metaphysical poets.*

Creeley, Robert: see *Black Mountain School.*

Cromwell, Oliver: see *Restoration comedy.*

Cullen, Countee: see *Harlem Renaissance.*

cultural materialism / cultural studies: The term "cultural materialism" was coined independently by anthropologist Marvin Harris (1927-2001) and cultural critic Raymond Williams

(1921-88)—and the term retains two distinct meanings. To be sure, there are points of similarity. In both anthropology and literary studies, cultural materialists define culture broadly; a television advertisement is as much a part of culture as is a performance of an opera or a play by Shakespeare. In both disciplines culture is regarded as inextricably linked to political-economic systems. And in both disciplines cultural materialism refuses the concept of cultural universality; anthropologists and cultural critics each found their own reasons to reject the presumptions of those who had maintained (as had Sir Arthur Quiller-Couch in 1918) that a "true classic [such as Shakespeare's *The Tempest*] is universal, in that it appeals to the catholic [i.e., universal] mind of man."

Despite the similarities, a cultural materialist in anthropology is quite a different thing from a cultural materialist in literary studies. In anthropology, cultural materialism does not presume any political stance; it has at its center efforts to explain sociocultural practices, especially those that may seem "irrational" (e.g., beliefs in witches, prohibitions against eating certain foods). Anthropologists find explanations for such practices in particular aspects of a society's economic and geographic conditions—and generally conclude that the seemingly irrational serves a useful social function.

Cultural materialism in literary studies, on the other hand, does presume a politically committed stance; it is strongly informed by Marxist thought. Whereas Marx focused on the production of physical goods, cultural materialists consider such things as ideology and narrative material—the so-called "superstructure" of society—also to be subject to principles of production. They are less interested in the physical products of culture—the book as a physical object, for example—than they are in the production of ideas. They focus much of their attention on the interplay between the dominant ideology and the ways in which resistance to that ideology is negotiated. Rather than trying to explain (or explain away) cultural phenomena through reference to particular economic phenomena, they resist fixed meanings, seeking to explore various ways in which dominant and subversive ideological strains may play out within particular texts (and to explore tensions and contradictions within the dominant ideology). They look both at texts' initial cultural production and at the ways their meanings may have been reconstructed in subsequent eras. They pay particular attention to issues of class, race, gender, and sexual orientation.

Raymond Williams's studies of eighteenth- to twentieth-century British culture are the founding works of cultural materialism; important subsequent figures include Catherine Belsey (b. 1940), Alan Sinfield (b. 1941), and Jonathan Dollimore (b. 1948). A good example of a cultural materialist approach to a text is Paul Brown's essay on *The Tempest* in Sinfield and Dollimore's *Political Shakespeare* (1985); Brown argues that Shakespeare's play is "radically ambivalent [with regard to] British colonialism in its initial phase." See also *new historicism*—an area of thought with which cultural materialism has close affinities.

Cultural materialism forms much of the base for cultural studies—a discipline in which the range both of material studied (more emphasis on popular culture, and on non-Western cultures) and of theories drawn on (Barthes, Kristeva, and others, as well as Marx and Williams) is expanded considerably beyond the common practice of cultural materialists.

cycle plays: See *biblical plays*.

dactyl: a metrical *foot* containing one strong stress followed by two weak stresses: / x x (e.g., "muttering," "helplessly"). A minor form known as *double dactyls* makes use of this meter (e.g., "higgledy piggledy"), often for humorous purposes.

d

Darwin, Charles: see *affect, Theory.*

de Kooning, Willem: see *expressionism / impressionism.*

dead metaphor: a *metaphor* that has been used so frequently that it no longer conjures up any physical image in the minds of those who hear it or read it. If we hear a politician say that something "paves the way for a better future," we do not think of actual paving—any more than we think of an actual bud when we hear that something with the potential to cause trouble should be "nipped in the bud."

death of the author: see *author.*

deconstruction: a theoretical and critical approach deriving from the ideas of various twentieth-century French thinkers—most notable among them Jacques Derrida (1930-2004). Derrida held that whatever we can say about a literary work (or indeed about any subject) is rooted in the unstable medium of language; to aim for "knowledge" of any permanent sort is pointless. It is far more fruitful, in Derrida's view, to conduct explorations that make no attempt to resolve difficulties or to reach any single conclusion, but aim rather to problematize—to raise doubts and uncertainties where all seemed clear, and to uncover difficulties and paradoxes where none were apparent.

defamiliarization: a term derived from the work of *Russian formalists* to describe art's capacity to render strange something that was previously familiar—to make us perceive a thing anew. See also *delayed decoding.*

Defoe, Daniel: see *novel, picaresque narrative.*

delayed decoding: a form of *defamiliarization* in which sense impressions are not decoded immediately, so that what is happening is at first only partially or imperfectly understood. The phenomenon was given this name by the critic Ian Watt (1917-99), who used the following passage from Joseph Conrad's *Heart of Darkness* (1902) as an example:

> I saw vague forms of men running bent double, leaping, gliding, distinct, incomplete, evanescent. Something big appeared in the air before the shutter, the rifle went overboard, and the man stepped back swiftly, looked at me over his shoulder in an extraordinary, profound, familiar manner, and fell upon my feet. The side of his head hit the wheel twice, and the end of what appeared a long cane clattered round and knocked over a little camp-stool. It looked as though after wrenching that thing from somebody ashore he had lost his balance in the effort.

Only later do both narrator and reader understand that the thing like a "long cane" was a spear, which has wounded the man standing near Marlow (the narrator).

Deleuze, Gilles: see *affect*.

Deloney, Thomas: see *novel*.

denotation: see *connotation*.

dénouement: the portion of a narrative that follows a dramatic crisis. In a dénouement, conflicts are resolved and the narrative is brought to a close. Traditional accounts of narrative structure often posit a triangle or arc, with rising action followed by a crisis and then by a dénouement. (Such accounts bear little relation, however, to the ways in which most actual narratives are structured—particularly most twentieth- and twenty-first-century literary fictions.) See also *Freytag's pyramid*.

d

Derain, André: see *expressionism / impressionism.*

Derrida, Jacques: see *animal studies, aporia, deconstruction, différance, logocentric, postmodernism, psychoanalytic criticism, structuralism / poststructuralism.*

descriptive: see *prescriptive.*

deus ex machina: a Latin term literally meaning "god from a machine," "deus ex machina" originally referred to the practice in ancient Greek and Roman theater of having a god appear onstage to solve a problem or resolve a conflict (the "machine" was a device used to lower the actor onto the stage from above). The term came to be used more generally to refer to any character or event that provides an unlikely or unforeseen means of solving an apparently unsolvable problem in a plot.

dialogue: words spoken by characters to one another. (When a character is addressing himself or herself or the audience directly, the words spoken are referred to as a *monologue.*)

diction: word choice. Of obvious importance to poetry, diction is also very important in other genres: whether the diction of a literary work (or of a literary character) is colloquial, conversational, formal, or of some other type contributes significantly to the tone of the text as well as to *characterization.*

didacticism: an aesthetic approach emphasizing moral instruction.

différance: a term coined by the French philosopher Jacques Derrida in 1963, and elaborated by him in subsequent writing. The written form is fundamental to the term. It is pronounced in the same way as the noun *différence* (meaning difference); the different spelling is a sign that we are to look for further meanings. Central to those meanings for Derrida were the two

d

different meanings of the French verb *différer*—to differ, and to postpone (or defer). Different but complementary aspects of both meanings go into the concept of *différance* as a means of expressing the ways in which meaning can never be stable and fixed. First, Derrida saw the meaning of any object or concept as being shaped not absolutely by anything intrinsic to the thing or concept itself. Rather it is shaped by the ways in which we see that object or concept in relation to other things—and in how the object or concept is perceived to differ from other objects or concepts. Second, Derrida saw words as always being inadequate to the task of giving complete expression to meaning: once one has made an attempt to express a meaning one must resort to further attempts, to more words; one must endlessly defer, and the moment when complete understanding of any meaning is achieved can never arrive.

dimeter: any poetic meter in which each line contains two *feet*. The following stanza is written in *iambic* dimeter (i.e., each line contains two iambic feet):

And all among	And all / a-mong
The joyful throng	The joy / ful throng
Burst out in song.	Burst out / in song.

Dionysian: see *Apollonian*.

dirge: a song or poem that mourns someone's death. See also *elegy* and *lament*.

discourse analysis: an umbrella term that may refer to a variety of approaches to analyzing speech and writing. As used by linguists, the term "discourse" denotes language units longer than a single sentence; one important form of discourse analysis involves the study of formal linguistic patterns across sentences, paragraphs, complete written works, entire conversations, and so

d

on. Such analyses may shed light on how patterns of discourse may vary, for example, according to the gender of the speaker (or writer); on the basis of class or cultural background; or in different academic disciplines. Among the leading figures in the broad category of linguistic discourse analysis are M.A.K. Halliday (b. 1925) and Teun A. van Dijk (b. 1943).

A second broad category of approach to discourse analysis is based not on the science of linguistics but on analyses of power relations as they are embedded in language and in discursive practice. A leading figure in discourse analysis of this sort has been the French theorist Michel Foucault (1926-84); according to Foucault, discursive practice is very largely shaped by its larger institutional context, which is charged with ideological content, embodying assumptions about the world that are often self-confirming to those operating within the particular institutions.

dissonance: harsh, unmusical sounds or rhythms that poets may use deliberately to achieve certain effects.

Donne, John: see *conceit, implied reader, metaphysical poets.*

Doolittle, Hilda (H.D.): see *Imagism.*

doppelgänger: German term for a literary double—someone in a fictional narrative who functions both as an independent character and as the alter ego of another character. In Joseph Conrad's "The Secret Sharer" (1909), for example, the character of Leggatt persuades the captain of a ship to let him hide on board; the captain feels a strong sense of connection to Leggatt, whose character seems in many ways to mirror his own.

double: see *doppelgänger.*

double dactyl: fixed poetic form in which lines of *dactylic dimeter* (i.e., lines composed of two dactyls each) figure prominently.

Poems written in this form must have two stanzas, each of four lines, with the last line of each stanza breaking with the "two dactyls" pattern and being formed instead by a *choriambus* (a *trochee* and an *iamb*). There are further requirements as well: the last lines of each stanza must rhyme, the first line of the poem must be made up of nonsense words (such as "higgledy piggledy" or "hickory dickory"), and the second line of the poem must name its subject, usually with one or more proper nouns. Though the double dactyl is generally thought of as a form of light verse, it may also have serious content—as in this example:

Daddybe daddybe
Bush who was president,
Son of the president:
Both fought Iraq.

Bombs fell obediently,
Soldiers obediently:
How many died and how
Many came back?

double rhyme: rhyme involving two syllables, usually with the first syllable stressed and the second unstressed (long referred to as "feminine rhyme"). The rhyme between "thinking" and "sinking" is a double rhyme, as is the rhyme between "hasty" and "tasty."

Dowland, John: see *asyndeton*.

dramatic irony: this form of *irony* occurs when the audience has access to information not available to one or more characters.

dramatic monologue / persona poem / dramatic poem: A dramatic monologue is a lyric poem that takes the form of an utterance by a single person addressing a silent or imagined listener. The speaker may be a historical personage (as in several of

Robert Browning's dramatic monologues), a figure drawn from myth or legend (as in some of Tennyson's), or an entirely fictional figure, as in Augusta Webster's "A Castaway" (1870).

More clearly focused definitions of the dramatic monologue specify not only that it be a poem written entirely in the voice of someone other than the poet, and a poem that is focused largely or entirely on revealing to the reader significant aspects of the character giving voice to the poem, but also that the poem suggest interaction with one or more other characters through clues in what the speaker says. Such clues may be given, for example, through passages in the second person (such as these in Robert Browning's "My Last Duchess" [1842]—"Will 't please you sit and look at her?," "Will 't please you rise?") or by phrasings that indicate the speaker is responding to something someone else has said (such as the question we presume has just been put to the speaker of Carol Ann Duffy's "Stealing" [1987] when the poem begins in this way: "The most unusual thing I ever stole? A snowman").

Broader definitions (such as that put forward by M.H. Abrams) suggest that a poem may be classed as a dramatic monologue even if it does not suggest direct interaction with one or more other characters—even imagined ones. But if the dramatic monologue is to be defined so loosely as that, it might be argued, the "dramatic" is effectively drained away, leaving little to distinguish the dramatic monologue from the monologue *per se*. Arguably, then, the more focused definition is the more useful one.

Those who prefer to define dramatic monologue in a more focused fashion but who feel it may be helpful to distinguish poems in which a persona is adopted in an extended fashion from, for example, monologues in a play, may find the term "persona poem" useful. This term may be used to denote poems that are written with one persona speaking throughout, regardless of whether the poems suggest through their phrasings the immediate presence of other people with whom the speaker is interacting. By this definition all dramatic monologues would be persona poems, but not all persona poems would be dramatic monologues.

A related category is the "dramatic poem." As the name suggests, a dramatic poem involves more than one character, presented in dialogue rather than through a monologue. Thomas Hardy's "The Ruined Maid" (1866) and Robert Frost's "The Death of the Hired Man" (1915) are well-known examples of dramatic poems.

dramatis personae: a Latin term literally meaning "people of the drama," "dramatis personae" refers to the characters in a work of fiction. It is sometimes used as the title for the list of a play's characters or cast.

dramaturgy / dramaturge: Dramaturgy is the art, theory, and technique of drama, and especially of dramatic composition. The term "dramaturge" refers sometimes to playwrights or directors, but it also may refer to a separate advisory role that can involve such tasks as choosing plays, editing new plays, and researching the historical context of older plays.

Dryden, John: see *allegory*.

dub poetry: a form of protest poetry originating in Jamaica, with its roots in dance rhythms, especially *reggae*, and often accompanied in performance by drums and music. See also *rap*.

Duffy, Carol Ann: see *apposition*, *dramatic monologue / persona poem / dramatic poem*, *occasional verse*.

duple foot: a duple foot of poetry has two syllables. The possible duple forms are *iamb* (in which the stress is on the second of the two syllables), *trochee* (in which the stress is on the first of the two syllables), *spondee* (in which both are stressed equally), and *pyrrhic* (in which both syllables are unstressed).

dystopia: see *Utopian literature.*

Eagleton, Terry: see *Marxist theory and criticism.*

eclogue: now generally used simply as an alternative name for a *pastoral* poem. In classical times and in the early modern period, however, an eclogue (or *idyll*) was a specific type of pastoral poem—a *dialogue* or *dramatic monologue* involving rustic characters. (The other main subgenre of the pastoral was the *georgic.*)

elegiac couplet: in the poetry of ancient Greece, a couplet frequently used in elegiac poetry and consisting of a hexameter line followed by a pentameter one, with a rhythm that rises in the first line and subsides in the second.

elegiac stanza: a *quatrain* of *iambic pentameters* rhyming *abab*, often used in poems meditating on death or sorrow. The name originated with Thomas Gray's "Elegy Written in a Country Churchyard" (1751); the form had until then been referred to as a heroic stanza.

elegy: poem of mourning. The word *elegy* comes from the Greek ε, λεγε ε, λεγε, usually translated as "Woe, cry woe, cry!" In ancient Greek poetry an elegy came to be regarded as having particular formal qualities—most particularly, to be written in *elegiac couplets*. As it has evolved in English poetry, however, the elegy is not tied to any particular form. John Milton's pastoral elegy "Lycidas" (1638) is written primarily in *iambic pentameter*; Thomas Gray's famous "Elegy Written in a Country Churchyard" (1751) is written in what was then known as heroic stanzas; Percy Shelley uses *Spenserian stanzas* in his "Adonais: An Elegy on the Death of John Keats" (1821); Alfred, Lord Tennyson, created a new stanza form for his *In Memoriam* (1850). The elegy in English literature may sometimes have at its heart a poetic cry of raw anguish at the death of a loved one, but more often than not it is a considered an expression of a wide range of thoughts and feelings occasioned by the death of a particular person. "Lycidas," "Elegy Written in a Country Churchyard," and *In Memoriam* are all composed of the poet's reflections on a variety of serious matters; they do not deal only with death, or only with the particular case of one individual who is being mourned.

The elegy in English literature may also vary widely in length—from the 16 lines of W.H. Auden's "Funeral Blues" (1940) to the more than 50 pages of *In Memoriam*. See also *dirge*, *pastoral elegy*.

Eliot, George: see *intrusive narrator*.

Eliot, T.S.: see *chorus*, *free verse*, *modernism*, *mythopoeic theory and criticism*, *New Criticism*.

elision: the omission or suppression of a letter or an unstressed syllable at the beginning or end of a word, so that a line of verse may conform to a given metrical scheme. For example, the three syllables at the beginning of Shakespeare's sonnet 129 are reduced to two by the omission of the first vowel: "Th' expense of spirit in a waste of shame." See also *syncope*.

Ellington, Duke: see *Harlem Renaissance*.

ellipsis: the omission of a word or words necessary for the complete grammatical construction of a sentence, but not necessary for our understanding of the sentence.

Elyot, Thomas: see *humanism / Renaissance humanism*.

embedded narrative: a story contained within another story.

Emerson, Ralph Waldo: see *Neo-Platonism*, *Transcendentalism*.

Empson, William: see *New Criticism*.

encomium: a literary work written to praise a person, a thing, or an occasion.

end: See *plot*.

end-rhyme: rhyme that operates at the end of lines (as opposed to *internal rhyme*). See also *rhyme*.

end-stopped: a line of poetry is said to be end-stopped when the end of the line coincides with a natural pause in the syntax, such as the conclusion of a sentence; e.g., in this couplet from Pope's "Essay on Criticism" (1711), both lines are end-stopped: "A little learning is a dangerous thing; / Drink deep, or taste not the Pierian spring." Compare this with *enjambment*.

Engels, Friedrich: see *Marxist theory and criticism*.

English sonnet: see *sonnet (Shakespearean)*.

enjambment: the running on of sense and grammatical construction from one line of poetry to the next. The resulting run-on lines are in contrast to *end-stopped* lines, in which the end of a phrase or clause (and the punctuation marking it, whether comma, period, or semi-colon) occurs at the end of a line. An example is provided by the first four lines of Robert Frost's sonnet "The Silken Tent," in which the enjambment helps to convey the billowing movement of the breeze: "She is as in a field a silken tent / At midday when a sunny summer breeze / Has dried the dew and all its ropes relent, / So that in guys it gently sways at ease...."

envoy (envoi): a stanza or half-stanza that forms the conclusion of certain French poetic forms, such as the *sestina* or the *ballade*. It often sums up or comments upon what has gone before.

epic: a lengthy narrative poem, often divided into books and sub-divided into *cantos*. It generally celebrates heroic deeds or events, and the style tends to be lofty and grand. Examples in English include Spenser's *The Faerie Queene* (1590s) and Milton's *Paradise Lost* (1667).

epic simile: an elaborate *simile*, developed at such length that the vehicle of the comparison momentarily displaces the primary subject with which it is being compared.

epigram: a succinct statement or a very short poem, sometimes in closed couplet form, characterized by pointed wit.

epigraph: a quotation placed at the beginning of a text to indicate or foreshadow the theme.

epiphany: a moment at which matters of significance are suddenly illuminated for a literary character (or for the reader), typically triggered by something small and seemingly of little import. The term first came into wide currency in connection with the fiction of James Joyce (1882-1941).

epiphora: see *epistrophe*.

episodic plot: a plot made up of episodes that are only loosely connected (as opposed to plots that present one or more continually unfolding narratives, with successive episodes building on one another). When a work is plotted episodically rather than as an Aristotelian whole (see *plot*), the reader or audience is given far less sense of causal connection, and far less material with which to form expectations of what is likely to happen.

epistolary novel: a novel made up of letters. Some epistolary novels consist entirely of letters by one character; most involve an exchange of letters between characters. The epistolary novel

e

enjoyed great popularity in the eighteenth century; Samuel Richardson's *Clarissa* (1748) and Frances Burney's *Evelina* (1778) are two of the best-known examples. Alice Walker's Pulitzer Prize-winning *The Color Purple* (1982) is one of the few epistolary novels of the past half-century to achieve wide recognition.

epistrophe / epiphora: a classical rhetorical device in which the same word or words are used to conclude a series of two or more poetic lines, sentences, or phrases. In this example from Walt Whitman's "Song of Myself" (1855-81), the repetitions of "myself" and "assume" are both instances of epistrophe: "I celebrate myself, and sing myself / And what I assume you shall assume."

epithalamion: a poem celebrating a wedding. The best-known example in English is probably Edmund Spenser's "Epithalamion" (1595).

epode: the third part of an *ode*, following the *strophe* and *antistrophe*.

Erasmus, Desiderius: see *humanism / Renaissance humanism*.

essay: a piece of prose non-fiction of limited length, written on a clearly defined topic. The essay has its roots in the writing of classical Rome—notably, in the *Moral Epistles* of the Roman philosopher Seneca (first century CE); its modern form was shaped by the sixteenth-century French writer Michel de Montaigne (1533-92), whose *essais* (literally, "attempts," or "tries") are personal reflections on a wide variety of broad topics ranging from marriage to education, and various aspects of current affairs.

essentialism: the view that particular types have in their identity something that is fundamental and unchanging. In the philosophy of Plato, all beings have an ideal form that constitutes their essential being; in modern discussions of gender, some have presumed there to be one or more characteristics that are essential to the nature of male and female—while others have argued that gender is socially constructed (and thus subject to change). The concept of essentialism has also been a frequent reference point in colonial and *postcolonial studies*; Edward Said (1935-2003) and others have commented on the tendency in Western thought to believe that different peoples (and different races) possess characteristics essential to their collective natures.

ethos: along with *logos* and *pathos*, one of the three categories of appeal that are set out in classical *rhetoric*. For Aristotle and other ancient Greek authorities, an appeal to ethos was one based on the character of the person presenting the argument—whether that might have to do with the speaker's position of authority, perceived honesty, or other ethical virtues. In modern usage, *ethos* is still used to refer to the character of the person putting forward an argument, but there may be different factors that come into play today in determining a sense of character.

eulogy: a text expressing praise, especially for a distinguished person recently deceased.

euphemism: mode of expression through which aspects of reality considered to be vulgar, crudely physical, or unpleasant are referred to indirectly rather than named explicitly. A variety of euphemisms exist for the processes of urination and defecation; "passed away" is often used as a euphemism for "died."

euphony: pleasant, musical sounds or rhythms—the opposite of *cacophony*.

euphuistic: rhetorically elaborate and heavily decorated with *figures of speech*. Coined with reference to John Lyly's prose narrative *Euphues* (1578). The term is now often used pejoratively to mean "excessively ornate or affected." Here is a sample from Lyly's original:

> The Sun shineth upon the dunghill, and is not corrupted; the diamond lieth in the fire, and is not consumed; the crystal toucheth the toad, and is not poisoned; the bird lieth by the mouth of the crocodile and is not spoiled; a perfect wit is never bewitched with lewdness, neither enticed with lasciviousness.

exegesis: detailed (usually line-by-line) explanation and/or interpretation of a text. The term is most frequently used with reference to the Bible, but it may refer to the close study of any text.

exemplum: a short and usually very simple story, told to illustrate a moral point—to provide an example in ethical instruction. Exempla were an important element in medieval sermons; they may also be found in literary works such as "The Nun's Priest's Tale" in Chaucer's *Canterbury Tales* (1387).

existentialism: a philosophical approach according to which the meaning of human life is derived from the actual experience of the living individual. The existential worldview, in which life is assumed to have no *essential* or pre-existing meanings, but to have only those meanings we personally choose to endow it with, can produce an *absurdist* sensibility.

exposition: the setting out of material in an ordered (and usually concise) form, either in speech or in writing.

In a play, those parts of the action that do not occur on stage but are rather recounted by the characters are frequently described as being presented in exposition. Similarly, when the background narrative is filled in near the beginning of a novel, such material is often described as having been presented in exposition.

In describing prose non-fiction, "exposition" can have two meanings. It can refer to prose intended to provide explanation; one way of classifying compositions is with the four (sometimes overlapping) categories of argumentation, description, exposition, and narration. But it may also be used more broadly; the term "expository prose" is often used to refer to essays or other works of prose non-fiction that may combine all of these four elements.

See also *Freytag's pyramid*.

expressionism / impressionism: Broadly understood, the term "expressionist" can be applied to any work of art that disregards conventions of *realism* in order to portray emotions or ideas more intensely. In visual art, expressionism is often contrasted with impressionism, another movement that took root in the late nineteenth century; whereas impressionists attempt to convey the impressions that the outer world makes on the human senses—most notably, visual perceptions—expressionists attempt to give outward expression to sensations they feel within themselves. Though expressionism is strongly associated with a diverse and influential *avant-garde* movement that occurred in Germany in the first quarter of the twentieth century, the most widely referenced works of expressionist visual art may well be the several paintings and drawings that Norwegian artist Edvard Munch completed between 1893 and 1910, each one entitled *The Scream*. The early-twentieth-century work of the painters known collectively as Les Fauves (The Wild Beasts) has also been associated with expressionism—though this is one of many areas where the line between expressionism and impressionism may begin to blur. Just as our inward feelings may influence the way we receive impressions of the world, so too the line between impressionism and expressionism may be difficult to locate. Should the early-twentieth-century work of the Fauve painter André Derain (1880-1954) be labeled post-impressionist or expressionist? Or neither, or both? Similar questions may be asked of the art of Vincent Van Gogh (1853-90), or that of Oskar Kokoshka (1886-1980).

Early-twentieth-century German visual artists such as Wassily Kandinsky (1866-1944) and Ernst Ludwig Kirchner (1880-1938) decried realism and rationalism in the arts, embraced anti-bourgeois ideals of social and spiritual transformation—and, in Kandinsky's case, saw art as being grounded in an "inner necessity" that eventually led him toward purely abstract compositions. Later-twentieth- and twenty-first-century expressionists in the visual arts include Georges Rouault (1871-1958) in France, Egon Schiele (1890-1918) in Germany, Francis Bacon (1909-92) and Lucian Freud (1922-2011) in Britain, and Willem de Kooning (1904-97) in the United States. The mid-century movement among American artists such as Mark Rothko (1903-70) and Helen Frankenthaler (1928-2011), known as Abstract Expressionism, which takes leave entirely of the representational, has strong roots in the work of Kandinsky and other German artists.

If expressionist painting is often characterized by the use of striking colors and simplified or distorted forms, expressionist literature is often characterized by non-realistic elements such as extreme simplification of form, intensity of language and of emotion, the use of archetypes, and the abandonment of linearity and logic. The influence of expressionism in literature has been stronger in drama than in fiction or poetry; the expressionist tradition in drama includes the late-nineteenth- and early-twentieth-century work of Swedish playwright August Strindberg (1849-1912), early-twentieth-century work by Kokoshka and Kandinsky (both of whom were dramatists as well as painters), several early-twentieth-century plays by the American Eugene

O'Neill (1888-1953), Max Frisch's *The Arsonists* (1953; original title *Biedermann und die Brandstifter*), and some of the later work of the British dramatist Caryl Churchill (b. 1938).

Discussions of impressionism in literature, on the other hand, have focused far more on fiction and poetry than on drama. Analogues to the efforts made by impressionist painters to represent sense impressions have been located in the way in which certain authors use imagery. The *delayed decoding* of some of the images in Joseph Conrad's *Heart of Darkness* (1902) is one oft-cited example. *Stream of consciousness* and *free indirect* styles of narrative in prose fiction have also sometimes been associated with impressionism—though it might well be argued that this is another of those areas where the line between expressionism and impressionism may begin to blur. *Imagism* in poetry has also often been associated with impressionism.

eye rhyme: rhyming that pairs words with similar spellings but dissimilar pronunciation: for example, "though" / "slough."

fable: a short *allegorical* tale that conveys an explicit moral lesson. The characters are often non-human animals or objects with human speech and mannerisms. See also *parable*.

falling action: see *Freytag's pyramid*.

falling rhythm: a pattern of rhythm in which syllables flow from stressed to unstressed; *trochaic* and *dactylic* meters tend to display this pattern. In English verse, falling rhythm is much less common than its opposite, *rising rhythm*, in which syllables flow from unstressed to stressed.

fantasy: in fiction, a subgenre characterized by the presence of magical or miraculous elements—usually acknowledged as such by the characters and the narrative voice. In *magic realism*, by contrast, miraculous occurrences tend to be treated by the characters and/or the narrative voice as if they were entirely ordinary. In fantasy (also in contrast to magic realism), the fictional world generally has an internal consistency to it that precludes any sense of absurdity on the part of the reader, and the plot tends to build a strong sense of expectation in the reader.

The subgenre of fantasy has expanded considerably since the landmark success of J.R.R. Tolkien's *The Lord of the Rings* in the 1950s, and it now encompasses a number of further divisions, from "epic fantasy" (the category that Tolkien's work did so much to define) and "Celtic fantasy" to "urban fantasy" and *steampunk*. The greatest success in twenty-first-century fantasy literature— J.K. Rowling's Harry Potter series—resists easy categorization under any of these terms.

farce: form of broad *comedy* in which the humor is dependent on elements such as physicality, sight gags, and confused identities.

Faulkner, William: see *grotesque*.

feminine ending: the ending of a line of poetry on an "extra," and, especially, on an unstressed syllable. See, for example, the first line of Keats's "Ode on a Grecian Urn" (1819): "A thing of beauty is a joy forever," a line of iambic pentameter (A thing / of beau- / ty is / a joy / for-e-ver) in which the final foot is an *amphibrach* rather than an *iamb*. An alternative term is "soft landing."

feminine rhyme: see *double rhyme; rhyme*.

feminism / feminist criticism and theory / gender-based criticism and theory: In literary study, the term "feminist" is applied to analyses that attend to the lives and perspectives of women and/or to gender inequality and gender difference in literary texts and the societies in which they were produced. Many people feel that in academic disciplines such as literary studies, feminism is less a matter of taking a different methodological approach than it is of what one notices, or what one asks questions about—entirely a matter of content, in short, rather than of process. But like other questions as to the nature of feminism, that contention is disputed; some feel that there are a range of methodologies that have natural affinities with feminist ideas. Certainly it may be said that some tendencies seem to cut across many different forms of feminism. One is a tendency to value personal experience as a legitimate source of knowledge and to question beliefs that are widely held as "common sense" or "objective truth." (Such an approach is considered necessary because "objective truth" was until recently constructed almost entirely by males and rested in no small part on the assumption that male superiority was among the most objective and permanent of truths.) A second is a tendency to resist *binary* oppositions such as male and female, or reason and emotion; though arguments concerning the social construction of gender or the necessary interdependence of reason and emotion in human thought are not inherently feminist, they are consistent with the approach taken by most forms of feminism in recent generations.

That there are many forms of feminism (or "feminisms," as they are sometimes called) has become a truism, but it is nonetheless true. Historians often apply the term "first-wave feminism" to the approach of late-nineteenth- and early-twentieth-century suffragists and other activists—and use the same label to describe the early-twentieth-century literary criticism of Virginia Woolf (1882-1941) and others. "Second-wave feminism" is a term applied to the 1960s through 1980s. In literary studies, the ground-breaking work of Sandra Gilbert (b. 1936) and Susan Gubar (b. 1944), and of Anne K. Mellor (b. 1941) that dates from this period employs many of the same critical methodologies as male literary critics of the previous half-century had done. But by asking different questions and taking different lines of approach, critics such as Gilbert and Gubar and Mellor saw radically different things and reached radically different conclusions than had their predecessors about texts such as *Frankenstein* and *Jane Eyre*. Subsequent feminist criticism has taken a variety of different forms, often linked to, but also in tension with, methodologies such as *poststructuralist* theory (Luce Irigaray, Julia Kristeva, Hélène Cixous), *new historicism* (Judith Newton, Carol Thomas Neely), *postmodernism* and *queer theory* (Judith Butler, Eve Kosofsky Sedgwick), and *postcolonial theory* and criticism (Gayatri Spivak, bell hooks).

A further complication in using the term "feminism" is the danger of *anachronism*; if one uses twentieth- or twenty-first-century terminology (the term "feminist" did not come into common use until well into the twentieth century) to describe the attitudes of writers from centuries earlier, confusion may often result. May an eighteenth-century advocate of rights for women be legitimately described as a feminist? Should we resort to the term "protofeminist"? Or is that to sow further confusion, conveying a false impression of inevitability about history? Is it legitimate to discuss a text such as the twelfth-century *Lais* of Marie de France (many of which have a strongly female focus, and implicitly challenge many of the oppressive practices of the time) as in some sense feminist? Some argue that the term "feminist" should always be avoided in such contexts; others regard it as quite acceptable to use the term as a reference point in discussions of earlier periods, provided one does so with sensitivity to the historical reality, and not in a way that imposes today's expectations on bygone eras).

Many critics and theorists today are more comfortable speaking of "gender-based approaches to literature" than of feminist approaches; one welcome development in the critical and theoretical practice of the past generation has been the broadening of the various approaches taken in feminist criticism to include insights into the role of the male in the literatures of different eras and different cultures. It is likely that specifically feminist approaches will continue to have an important role to play, however—at least for as long as we live in societies in which it remains commonplace to refer to all human beings as "mankind"—or to describe first-year students as "freshmen."

Ficino, Marsilio: see *Neo-Platonism*.

fiction: imagined or invented narrative. In literature, the term is usually used to refer to prose narratives (such as novels and short stories).

Fielding, Henry: see *intrusive narrator, picaresque narrative*.

figures of speech: expressions in which language is employed deliberately and generally in highly concentrated form, in order to achieve particular purposes or effects on an audience. There are two kinds of figures: schemes and *tropes*. Schemes involve changes in word-sound and word-order, such as *alliteration* and *chiasmus*. Tropes play on our understandings of words to extend, alter, or transform meaning, as in *metaphor* and *personification*.

first-person narrative: a narrative recounted using *I* and *me*. See also *narrative perspective*.

Fish, Stanley: see *reader response criticism / reader response theory*.

fixed forms: a term applied to a number of poetic forms and stanzaic patterns, many derived from French models, such as *ballade, rondeau, sestina, triolet*, and *villanelle*. Other fixed forms include the *sonnet, rhyme royal, haiku*, and *ottava rima*.

flashback: in fiction, the inclusion of a scene (or scenes) from an earlier point in time relative to the primary thread of a story's narrative. Flashbacks may be used to revisit from a different viewpoint events that have already been recounted in the main thread of narrative; to present material that had been left out in the initial recounting; or to present relevant material from a time before the beginning of the main thread of narrative. The use of flashbacks in fiction is sometimes referred to as *analepsis*.

flashforward: the inclusion of a scene (or scenes) from a later point in time relative to the primary thread of a story's narrative. See also *prolepsis*.

flat character: the opposite of a *round character*, a flat character is defined by a small number of traits and does not possess enough complexity to be psychologically realistic. "Flat character" can be a disparaging term, but need not be; flat characters serve different purposes in a fiction than round characters, and are often better suited to some types of literature, such as allegory or farcical comedy.

Foer, Jonathan Safran: see *animal studies*.

foil: in literature, a character whose behavior and/or qualities set in relief for the reader or audience those of a strongly contrasting character who plays a more central part in the story.

Foley, John Miles: see *oral tradition*.

folio: large book size. For a folio-sized book, each large sheet of paper is folded only once, so as to form two leaves (four pages). The size of folio-sized books varies depending on the size of the sheets used; the most famous of all folio-sized books is the 1623 First Folio of Shakespeare's plays, which measures 8½ x 13⅜ inches.

foot: a unit of a line of verse which contains a particular combination of stressed and unstressed syllables. Dividing a line into metrical feet (*iambs*, *trochees*, etc.), and then counting the number of feet per line, is part of *scansion*. See also *meter*.

forced rhyme: see *rhyme*.

foreshadowing: the inclusion of elements in a story that hint at some later development(s) in the same story. For example, in Flannery O'Connor's short story "A Good Man Is Hard to Find" (1955), the old family burial ground that the family sees on their drive foreshadows the violence that follows.

foreword: a piece of introductory writing that appears before the main body of text of a book, and is generally written by someone other than the author(s) of the body of the book. (Note that a *fore*word appears be*fore* the other words in a book; the word "foreword" is not to be confused with the word "forward.")

formalist: In literary criticism, a term that may refer to any one of a number of approaches that emphasize the formal qualities of literary works (e.g., rhythm in poetry, narrative viewpoint in prose fiction). Formalism fell out of fashion beginning in the 1970s and for several decades was often disparaged for paying insufficient attention to broader concerns (ideology, historical circumstance, etc.). A branch of critical inquiry known as *new formalism* has aimed since the late 1990s to engage in formal literary analysis in ways that connect form with those broader concerns. (There is no direct connection between this new formalism among scholars and critics of literature and the new formalism movement among poets who have advocated a revival of traditional verse forms—and a corresponding de-emphasis on free verse.) See also *Russian formalism*.

Foucault, Michel: see *author, discourse analysis, postmodernism, queer theory, structuralism / poststructuralism.*

found space: a site that is not normally a theater but is used for the staging of a theatrical production. Often, the choice of found space can reflect the play's setting or thematic content.

frame narrative: a narrative that holds another narrative (or other narratives) enclosed within it. From Chaucer's *Canterbury Tales* (1387) to Shelley's *Frankenstein* (1818) to Conrad's *Heart of Darkness* (1902), frame narratives, together with the "story within the story" that they enclose, have figured prominently in English literature.

Francione, Gary: see *animal studies.*

Frankenthaler, Helen: see *expressionism / impressionism.*

Frazer, James: see *mythopoeic theory and criticism.*

free indirect style / free indirect discourse: a style of third-person narration that takes on some of the characteristics of *first-person narration*; in a passage written in free indirect style, the narrative typically assumes the perspective of a particular character or characters. When we hear through the third-person narrative voice of Jane Austen's *Pride and Prejudice* (1813), for example, that Mr. Darcy "was the proudest, most disagreeable man in the world, and everybody hoped that he would never come there again," the narrative voice has assumed the point of view of "everybody in the community"; we as readers are not meant to take it that Mr. Darcy is indeed the most disagreeable man in the world. Similarly, in the following passage from James Joyce's "The Dead" (1914), we are meant to take it as being the view of the character Gabriel that Miss Ivors "had no right to call him a West Briton" and had "tried to make him ridiculous," not to take it as an objective statement of truth on the part of the novel's third-person narrative voice:

> Gabriel tried to banish from his mind all memory of the unpleasant incident with Miss Ivors. Of course the girl or woman, or whatever she was, was an enthusiast but there was a time for all things. Perhaps he ought not to have answered her like that. But she had no right to call him a West Briton before people, even in joke. She had tried to make him ridiculous before people, heckling him and staring at him with her rabbit's eyes.

The inclusion here of phrases such as "he thought that" ("But he thought that she had no right to ...") would have the effect of making the *narrative perspective* more plain to the reader—but it would also make the prose less immediate in its tone, and more wordy.

The use of free indirect discourse allows the writer to move back and forth between the perspective of one or more of the characters and an omniscient perspective, to alternate among a variety of narrative perspectives, or to create uncertainty as to the narrative perspective; the term "free indirect discourse" is also sometimes applied to situations in which it may not be entirely clear if the thoughts expressed emanate from the character, the narrator, or some combination of the two.

free verse: poetry that does not follow any regular patterning of meter, line length, or sound (*rhyme*, *alliteration*, etc.). It is often maintained that no verse is entirely free—by which may be meant one of two things. The first is the idea that to write good free verse the poet will need to strive to make it musical; this idea stems from the early-twentieth-century proclamations of Ezra Pound (1885-1972) and T.S. Eliot (1888-1965), who advocated that poetry be "composed in the sequence of the musical phrase, not in the sequence of a metronome" (Pound) and averred that no verse is truly free "for the man [sic] who wants to do a good job" (Eliot). Others have suggested that to some extent rhythm and musicality are built into the language—that free verse will inevitably follow the complex natural "rules" and rhythmic patterns (or cadences) of speech.

Freud, Lucian: see *expressionism / impressionism*.

Freud, Sigmund: see *Freudian theory and criticism, psychoanalytic criticism, the uncanny*.

Freudian theory and criticism: literary theory and criticism inspired by, or in the tradition of, the work of Sigmund Freud (1856-1939), the founder of psychoanalysis. See also *psychoanalytic criticism*.

Freytag, Gustav: see *Freytag's pyramid, narratology / narrative theory*.

Freytag's pyramid: a model of plot structure developed by the German novelist, playwright, and critic Gustav Freytag and introduced in his book *Die Technik des Dramas* (1863). In the pyramid, five stages of plot are identified as occurring in the following order: *exposition*, rising action, climax, falling action, and *dénouement*. Freytag intended his pyramid to diagram the structure of classical five-act plays, but it is also used as a tool to analyze other forms of fiction (even though most individual plays and stories do not follow the structure outlined in the pyramid).

Frisch, Max: see *expressionism / impressionism*.

Frost, Robert: see *conceit, dramatic monologue / persona poem / dramatic poem, enjambment*.

Frye, Northrop: see *mythopoeic theory and criticism, Theory*.

full rhyme: see *rhyme.*

futurism: As an adjective, "futurist" is often used with a very general denotation; a writer's "futurist vision" may simply mean a vision oriented toward the future. As a noun, however, "futurism" denotes a specific movement in the history of ideas—one that emerged in Italy in the early years of the twentieth century. The futurists aimed toward a very specific sort of future—one in which technology and industry would play a leading role, in which the clean and dynamic lines of modern art and architecture would sweep away dusty traditions of ornamentation, and in which nationalist attachments and powerful leaders would flourish; the movement had a strong influence on the growth of the fascist movement in Italy. The futurists also influenced literature and visual art in English—notably the *Vorticism* of Ezra Pound (1885-1972), Wyndham Lewis (1882-1957), and others.

García Márquez, Gabriel: see *magic realism.*

gender-based criticism and theory: see *feminism.*

Genette, Gérard: see *narratology / narrative theory.*

genre: a class or type of literary work. The concept of genre may be used with different levels of generality. At the most general, poetry, drama, prose fiction, and literary non-fiction may be distinguished as separate genres. At a lower level of generality various subgenres are frequently distinguished, such as (within the genre of prose fiction) the novel, the novella, and the short story; and, at a still lower level of generality, the mystery novel, the detective novel, the novel of manners, and so on.

genre fiction: prose fiction that falls into one of several clearly recognizable categories, among them detective, *fantasy*, *science fiction*, mystery, *romance*, horror, and Western. Works classified as

g

genre fiction are more powerfully governed by conventions than are, for example, contemporary works of literary fiction; lovers must be united at the end of a romance novel, the identity of the murderer must be revealed near the end of a mystery novel, and so on.

georgic: a poem that celebrates the natural wealth of the countryside and provides advice as to how to cultivate and live in harmony with it. Pope's *Windsor Forest* (1713) and James Thomson's *Seasons* (1726-30) are classed as georgics. This form is a type of *pastoral poetry*; the *eclogue* is another.

The term "georgic" derives from the Greek verb meaning "to farm" and from Virgil's long poem *Georgics* (c. 30 BCE) on the theme of farming.

ghazal: derived from Persian and Indian precedents, the ghazal presents a series of thoughts (typically on the subject of love) in closed couplets, usually joined by a simple rhyme scheme such as *aa ba ca da, ab bb cb eb fb*, etc.

Gilbert, Sandra: see *feminism / feminist criticism and theory / gender-based criticism and theory.*

Gilman, Charlotte Perkins: see *closure.*

Ginsberg, Allen: see *Beat Writing.*

glosa: a poetic fixed form that originated in Spain during the *Renaissance*. In a glosa, the opening (the *cabeza*, or *texte*) is made up of a stanza (usually four lines) of a pre-existing poem; four stanzas then follow, each of ten lines, and each ending with one of the four lines of the text being glossed. These four stanzas comprise the body of the poem (also known as the *glosa proper* or *glose*). P.K. Page's *Hologram* (1994) was a widely discussed late-twentieth-century collection of glosas.

gloss: a brief note explaining the meaning of a word or phrase. In the case of classical works in Greek or Latin, glosses were often inserted between the lines; nowadays they normally appear in the margin or in footnotes.

gnomic verses: loosely linked proverbial sayings in verse form, presented as being of moral significance or otherwise meaningful. The term comes from the Greek word meaning "opinion." Ancient examples include Hesiod's *Works and Days* (eighth century BCE) and the biblical book of Proverbs; the verses from the Anglo-Saxon Cotton manuscript (c. tenth century) known as the Cotton Maxims or Gnomic Verses are an important medieval example.

Goethe, Johann Wolfgang von: see *Neo-Platonism*.

Gothic: in architecture and the visual arts, a term used to describe styles prevalent from the twelfth to the fourteenth centuries, but in literature a term used to describe work with a sinister or grotesque tone that seeks to evoke a sense of terror on the part of the reader or audience. Gothic literature originated as a genre in the eighteenth century with works such as Horace Walpole's *The Castle of Otranto* (1764). To some extent the notion of the medieval itself then carried with it associations of the dark and the grotesque, but from the beginning an element of intentional exaggeration (sometimes verging on self-parody) attached itself to the genre. The Gothic trend of youth culture that began in the late twentieth century is less clearly associated with the medieval, but shares with the various varieties of Gothic literature (from Walpole in the eighteenth century, to Bram Stoker in the early twentieth, to Stephen King and Anne Rice in the late twentieth) a fondness for the sensational and the grotesque, as well as a propensity to self-parody.

g

Gowdy, Barbara: see *animal studies*.

Grand, Sarah: see *New Woman literature*.

graphic literature: literature in which visual material is an integral element throughout. Some graphic literature may be entirely in visual form, but most combines the graphic with the verbal, most commonly in a series of frames. Although the term "graphic novel" is sometimes used loosely to describe the entire genre of graphic literature, not all graphic literature is novelistic in form; for example, many distinguished works of graphic literature— e.g., Art Spiegelman's *Maus* (1986), Alison Bechdel's *Fun Home* (2006), and Sarah Leavitt's *Tangles* (2010)—have been memoirs.

Graves, Robert: see *mythopoeic theory and criticism*.

Gray, Erik: see *invitation poem*.

Gray, Thomas: see *elegy, elegiac stanza, tail-rhyme*.

Greek literature: see *anagnorisis, antistrophe, Apollonian, catharsis, chorus, comedy, deus ex machina, elegy, elegiac couplet, ethos, georgic, hamartia, Hellenic / Hellenistic, humanism / Renaissance humanism, logos, lyric, mimesis, muse, nemesis, ode, oral tradition, orchestra, palimpsest, pastoral, pathos, peripeteia, poetic justice, poetics, proscenium, quantitative meter, rhetoric, Sapphic, strophe, theater-in-the-round, tragedy*.

Greenblatt, Stephen: see *historicism / new historicism*.

grotesque: Literature of the grotesque is characterized by a focus on extreme or distorted aspects of human characteristics—a focus that can serve to comment on and challenge societal norms. The term can also refer particularly to a character who is odd or disturbing. Writers associated with the grotesque include Flannery O'Connor (1925-64), Edgar Allan Poe (1809-49), and William Faulkner (1897-1962).

g

Gubar, Susan: see *feminism / feminist criticism and theory / gender-based criticism and theory*.

H.D. (Hilda Doolittle): see *Imagism*.

hagiography: in its original meaning, the genre of work that records in written form and in reverential tone the lives of Christian saints. This word is now commonly used pejoratively to describe biographical writing that treats its subject with excessive reverence—as if he or she were a saint.

haiku: Japanese poetic form, using three unrhymed lines. Conventionally, it uses precise, concentrated images to suggest states of feeling. In its traditional form a Japanese haiku includes precisely 17 phonetic sounds (known as *on*, or *morae*). Though these are not equivalent to English syllables, the haiku is often taught in English as a fixed form of seventeen syllables: five in the first line, seven in the second, five in the third. The following example is a loose translation of a haiku by the seventeenth-century Japanese poet Matsuo Bashō (c. 1644-94):

> on the leafless branch
> a dark crow makes no quick move
> autumn dusk falling

In English literature, the haiku became influential in the twentieth century, particularly in connection with *Imagism*.

half-rhyme: see *rhyme*.

Halliday, M.A.K.: see *discourse analysis*.

hamartia: From the Greek word meaning "error," a hamartia is a mistake that leads to the ruin of a *protagonist* in a *tragedy*. Aristotle developed the concept in his *Poetics*.

Hammett, Dashiell: see *noir*.

h

Haraway, Donna: see *animal studies*.

hard landing: see *masculine ending*.

Hardy, Thomas: see *dramatic monologue / persona poem / dramatic poem*, *quantity*.

Harlem Renaissance: period in the 1920s and 1930s of notable cultural achievement by African-American writers, intellectuals, artists, and musicians (among them the writers Countee Cullen, Langston Hughes, Zora Neale Hurston, Nella Larsen, and Jean Toomer; and the musicians Duke Ellington, Jelly Roll Morton, and Fats Waller), concentrated in the Harlem neighborhood of New York.

headless line: in poetry with a regular *meter*, a line of poetry in which the first *foot* is missing its first syllable. In *iambic* poetry a foot consists of an unstressed syllable followed by a stressed syllable; in the following four lines of iambic verse the third line is headless (i.e., its first foot consists of only one syllable):

> If you / look close / at all / these love- / ly blooms
> I know / you'll be / sur- prised. / What's that? / What zooms?
> Bird / that hov- / ers hum- / ing in / the air
> Is here, / is gone, / so fast / you know / not where.

A headless line may also be referred to as an "acephalous line."

Heaney, Seamus: see *synaesthesia*.

Hegel, G.W.F.: see *historicism / new historicism*.

Hellenic / Hellenistic: In its most general meaning, "Hellenistic" simply means having to do with Greece ("Hellas")—especially, as the term is commonly used, with ancient Greece. It is also conventional, however, to apply the term "Hellenistic period" to the last of the three periods into which ancient Greek history is commonly divided—the archaic (or Homeric) period, lasting until the early fifth century BCE; the classical period (also known as the Hellenic period), during which dramatists such as Sophocles and Aristophanes, philosophers such as Plato and Aristotle, and historians such as Herodotus and Thucydides all flourished; and the post-classical, or Hellenistic, period, which is known less for its literature than for its art, especially its sculpture. The Hellenistic period is typically placed in the time between the death of Alexander the Great in 323 BCE and the emergence of Rome as the dominant Mediterranean power in 31 BCE.

heptameter: a line containing seven metrical *feet*.

Herbert, George: see *metaphysical poets*, *pattern poetry*.

hermeneutics: the study of the meanings of texts, and of how they are interpreted. Applied originally to biblical *exegesis*, "hermeneutics" has become a term widely applied in literary studies and aesthetics. Can texts have fixed meanings, or must meaning be relative (varying according to different cultures, different eras, etc.)? To what extent should the meaning(s) intended by the author have standing in the interpretation of a text? To what extent is meaning constructed by the reader? These are some of the core questions of hermeneutics.

heroic couplet: a pair of rhymed *iambic pentameters*, so called because the form was much used in seventeenth- and eighteenth-century poems and plays on heroic subjects.

heroic stanza: see *elegiac stanza*.

Hesiod: see *gnomic verses*.

hexameter: a line containing six metrical *feet*.

h

hip-hop: a term describing primarily urban African-American youth culture, applied in music and verse to heavily rhythmic lyrics chanted to musical accompaniment. Hip-hop is often controversial in its choice of topics such as drugs, violence, and sex. See also *dub poetry*, *rap*, and *reggae*.

Hippocrates: see *aphorism*.

historical present: use of the present tense in a narrative set in the past. In the nineteenth century and through most of the twentieth the historical present was used by few writers of fiction, and those who did use it tended to do so only selectively, to lend a sense of immediacy to particular scenes. In the late twentieth century the use of the historical present in fiction became much more common, with many writers composing entire novels in the historical present.

The historical present is also frequently used in non-fiction—for example, by some writers of popular history.

historicism / new historicism: Whereas the verb "historicize" has a straightforward meaning—to look at something in its historical context(s)—the noun "historicism" is a term with several related but distinct meanings (including in art history and in theology as well as in philosophy, the social sciences, and the study of literature). The term may certainly be used to refer to *any* approach that favors taking historical context into account; in practice, however, it has often been used with reference to those influenced by the theories of history and of social development espoused by G.W.F. Hegel (1770-1831), Auguste Comte (1798-1857), and Karl Marx (1818-83). In the abstract it might reasonably be thought that a historicist approach, in being sensitive to historical context, would be more likely to be relativist than absolutist in nature. But the association of historicism with the thought of figures such as Comte and Marx (one feature of which was a tendency to postulate immutable laws according to which societies develop) has led some critics of this form of historicism—the philosopher Karl Popper (1902-94) most notable among them—to associate historicism with the belief that humans may use the raw materials of history to foretell the future—and engineer social outcomes in the light of the predictions history helps us to make.

The association of historicism with Marxist thought has sometimes been made in literary studies too—though it has also been common to apply the term "literary historicism" to a variety of non-Marxist approaches. Broadly, any approach to literature that takes historical context to be relevant to the interpretation of a literary work may be termed historicist. But are all form(s) of historical context equally relevant? Historicist approaches to English literature of the late nineteenth and early twentieth centuries often took an author's biographical background and certain sorts of cultural trends—especially in the history of ideas—to be particularly important. (It was largely in reaction to the perceived excesses of this sort of historicism that the mid-twentieth-century *New Critics* began to focus on the text itself, and to treat biographical and cultural background as extraneous to the business of the literary critic.) The historicist approaches of some other twentieth-century literary critics, however, took the historical context of social class, and of gender and race relations, to be particularly important.

Just as the New Criticism had arisen largely in reaction to the perceived excesses of biographical and cultural historicism, new historicism arose in the 1980s largely in reaction to a perceived failure of the New Criticism to take adequate account either of history or of ideology. The term "new historicism" was coined in 1982 by Stephen Greenblatt (in the context of discussing the

h

"mutual permeability" of the literary and the historical in studying Shakespeare and the Elizabethan period). A tendency to try to break down barriers between literary and non-literary texts has remained a feature of new historical approaches—as has a particular sensitivity to the material manifestations of culture, and a tendency toward uncovering assumptions relating to class, gender, race, and ideology that are embedded within a text but that may not be readily apparent to the reader. While new historicist literary approaches have been influenced by Marxist tradition in the attention they pay to economic and class relations, and to the material generally, they have tended to resist any notion that there can be immutable truths of history, or unchanging aspects either to individual cultures or to human nature as a whole. In their style of inquiry, new historicists do not generally engage in systematic empirical enquiry of the sort practiced by academic historians; they tend rather to follow suggestive connections and to particularly value the telling detail that may be used to suggest a much broader cultural reality.

Homer: see *author, Hellenic / Hellenistic, humanism / Renaissance humanism, oral tradition.*

homonym / homophone / homograph: Homonyms have different meanings but the same spelling or sound. There are thus two types of homonyms: homophones (e.g., "sight" and "site") have the same sound but different spellings, while homographs (e.g., "slough" meaning "swampy area," pronounced "*sloo*," and "slough" meaning "shed tissue," pronounced "*sluff*") have the same spelling, though they are pronounced differently.

hooks, bell: see *feminism / feminist criticism and theory / gender-based criticism and theory.*

Hopkins, Gerard Manley: see *sprung rhythm.*

h

Horace: see *carpe diem, Horatian ode, ode.*

Horatian ode: inspired by the work of the first-century BCE Roman poet Horace, an ode that is usually calm and meditative in tone, and homostrophic (i.e., having regular stanzas) in form. Keats's odes are English examples.

Housman, A.E.: see *catalexis, hyperbole.*

Hughes, Langston: see *Harlem Renaissance.*

humanism / Renaissance humanism: Nowadays the word "humanist" is often used to imply a "secular" opposition to religion in general and Christianity in particular. The opposite is the case with *Renaissance* humanism, particularly north of Italy. Humanists were distinguished from other scholars not by their exclusive focus on human or secular texts, but rather by their focus on both secular writings, particularly classical ones, and religious texts and thought. Thus the Renaissance scholar Erasmus produced books on Greco-Roman culture and an edition of the New Testament in the original Greek. In one key particular, humanism was in accord with Protestant thought: Erasmus and many other humanists supported making the Bible available in the vernacular. But—as attested by Thomas More's willingness to die rather than approve England's separation from the Roman Catholic Church—humanists tended to be more willing than Martin Luther or, later, John Calvin to remain connected to Roman Catholic tradition.

The recovery and reappraisal of works from classical Greece and Rome was central to Renaissance humanism—as it had been to medieval scholasticism centuries earlier. The recovery of texts by the scholastics, however, had stressed applying classical learning to theological ends, emphasized Aristotle's works, and tended to treat classical writings as authoritative. For Renaissance humanists, classical writings were of interest for many purposes: the epic poems of Homer and Virgil and the erotic poems of Ovid were of as much interest as the writings of the philosophers. And many humanists felt little obligation to demonstrate that a seemingly new idea in fact accorded with ancient authority. Renaissance humanism was often prepared to break new ground, and to acknowledge breaking it.

Of the Greek philosophers, Plato, rather than Aristotle, came to the fore in the Renaissance. Of particular importance was the Platonic concept of ideal forms—the notion that for every physical object, metaphysical concept, and ethical principle there is an ideal abstract form that in fact is more "real" than its manifestations in the actual or material world. It is not difficult to see how Platonic "ideas" could be harmonized with Christian ideals, and many humanist thinkers endeavored to do just that. But Platonic philosophy also lent force to the sometime humanist impulse, particularly in Italy, to celebrate humanity itself, if not without reference to a Creator then with unprecedented emphasis on human potential and free will. (A groundbreaking text here was the *Oration on the Dignity of Man* (1486) by the Florentine writer Pico della Mirandola.) The supreme English Renaissance example of the possibility of imagining human society as a body independent of the workings of God is More's *Utopia* (1516), which imagines, although with a countering irony and ambivalence, the transformation of a culture through fundamentally different but entirely human-made social structures and practices.

Though scholars differ as to its extent and influence, most agree that Renaissance humanism helped transform sixteenth-century English literature. The poems of Sir Thomas Wyatt (1503-42), a member of Henry VIII's court who introduced the Petrarchan *sonnet* to English literature, show the impact of Renaissance humanism, as do prose works such as Sir Thomas

Elyot's *The Book of the Governor* (1531) and Roger Ascham's *The Schoolmaster* (1570).

Earlier notions of Renaissance humanism often assumed a top-down view of the period in which coherent intellectual movements were prime moving forces of socio-economic as well as political and cultural change. Recent scholars doubt that such movements in intellectual history are often quite so unified and coherent, believing that bottom-up change driven by socio-economic or religious forces may have at least as great an impact. Nevertheless, the concept of Renaissance humanism remains central to any discussion of the period.

Hurston, Zora Neale: see *Harlem Renaissance.*

hymn: a song, usually a religious one in praise of divinity. Literary hymns may praise more secular subjects.

hyperbole: a *figure of speech* (a *trope*) that deliberately exaggerates or inflates meaning to achieve particular effects, such as the irony in A.E. Housman's claim (from "Terence, This Is Stupid Stuff," 1896) that "malt does more than Milton can / To justify God's ways to man."

iamb: the most common metrical *foot* in English verse, containing one unstressed syllable followed by a stressed syllable: x / (e.g., "between," "achieve").

Ibsen, Henrik: see *problem play.*

idyll: traditionally, a short *pastoral* poem that idealizes country life, conveying impressions of innocence and happiness.

image: the recreation in words of objects perceived by the senses, sometimes thought of as "pictures," although other senses besides sight are involved. Besides this literal application, the term also refers more generally to the descriptive effects of figurative language, especially in *metaphor* and *simile*.

imagery: words or phrases about something within the physical world (an action, sight, sound, smell, taste, or touch) that illustrate something about a story's characters, settings, or situations. For example, the imagery of spring (budding trees, rain, singing birds) in Kate Chopin's short story "The Story of an Hour" (1894) reinforces the suggestions of death and rebirth in the plot and theme.

Imagism: a poetic movement that was popular mainly in the second decade of the twentieth century. The goal of Imagist poets—such as H.D. (Hilda Doolittle, 1886-1961) and Ezra Pound (1885-1972) in their early work—was to represent emotions or impressions through highly concentrated *imagery*.

imperfect rhyme: see *rhyme*.

implied author: see *narrator*.

implied reader: term given wide currency in literary studies in the late twentieth century by Wolfgang Iser (1926-2007) and other *reader response* theorists. Texts are written in the expectation that a certain sort of person will read them (or hear them). In the case of a scholarly paper in philosophy (which might include phrases such as "Russell and Wittgenstein both believed, of course, that ..."), the implied reader is an academic philosopher. In the case of John Donne's "No Man is an Island" sermon, the implied audience is an early-seventeenth-century member of the Church of England. But it is unclear who the implied reader is of Donne's sonnet "Batter My Heart, Three Person'd God," which is addressed not to any human reader, but to God. It is worth asking, therefore, whether cues for responding to a text exist for readers who are very different from the implied reader.

impressionism: see *expressionism / impressionism*.

improvisation: the seemingly spontaneous invention of dramatic dialogue and/or a dramatic plot by actors without the assistance of a written text.

in medias res: Latin: in the middle of things. When a plot is structured so that the action first seen by the reader or audience occurs in the middle of a story, the narrative is said to begin *in medias res*. See also *flashback*, *plot*.

In Memoriam stanza: a four-line stanza in *iambic tetrameter*, rhyming *abba*: the type of stanza used by Tennyson in his long poem *In Memoriam* (1833-50).

incantation: a chant or recitation of words that are believed to have magical power. A poem can achieve an "incantatory" effect through a compelling rhyme scheme and other repetitive patterns.

intentional fallacy: the notion that we may say anything meaningful as to the meaning(s) of a text on the basis of evidence drawn from outside the text as to what its author intended it to mean. The term "intentional fallacy" was coined by W.K. Wimsatt and Monroe Beardsley in a 1946 essay; writing at a time when biographical criticism was still widespread, they argued that a literary work becomes "detached from its author at birth and goes about the world beyond his [sic] power to intend about it and control it." Similar notions were put forward by Roland Barthes in his equally influential 1967 essay "La Mort de l'Auteur" ("The Death of the Author").

It is one thing to say that a text is independent of its author—that it is not and cannot be controlled by its author's intentions. Few people nowadays would disagree. But should the author's intentions be regarded as entirely irrelevant to any discussion of the meaning(s) of a text? Such questions continue to spark lively discussion.

interior monologue: the expression in speech (or in writing) of a character's inner thoughts and feelings. A *monologue* is any speech by a character not in actual conversation with another character; if a monologue is written as if another person were present, it is a *dramatic monologue*; if it is written so that we imagine the character speaking to himself or herself (as if in thought, rather than as if in conversation), it is an interior monologue. An interior monologue may take the form of a loose string of words that imitates the way thoughts are often strung together in the human mind; in that case it is a *stream of consciousness* interior monologue (such as occurs in the last chapter of Joyce's 1922 novel *Ulysses*—an uninterrupted presentation over some 40 pages of the thoughts of a single character). An interior monologue need not be written in a stream of consciousness style, however; interior monologues by Shakespeare's leading characters (such as Macbeth's "I have almost forgot the taste of fears" or Hamlet's "To be, or not to be") are usually written in syntactically complete sentences, and in *iambic pentameter*.

interlocking rhyme: see *rhyme*.

interlude: a short and often comical play or other entertainment performed between the *acts* of a longer or more serious work, particularly during the later Middle Ages and early *Renaissance*.

internal rhyme: rhyme that operates within lines of poetry (as opposed to at the ends of lines). See also *rhyme*.

intertextuality: the relationships between one literary work and other literary works. *Allusion*, imitation, *parody*, and *satire* are examples of intertextuality.

intrusive narrator: omniscient narrator who offers comments on the story (and/or on other matters) directly to the reader. The narrator of Henry Fielding's *Tom Jones* (1749) is famously intrusive: when he is about to introduce "Mr. Western's daughter" to the reader at the end of Book 3 of the novel, for example, he stops himself: "But this being the intended heroine of this work, a lady with whom we ourselves are greatly in love, and with whom many of our readers will probably be in love too, before we part, it is by no means proper she should make her appearance at the end of a book." Other authors who are known for intrusive narrators include Leo Tolstoy (1828-1910), Anthony Trollope (1815-82), and George Eliot (most notably, in Chapter 17 of her 1859 novel *Adam Bede*).

inversion: construction in which the normal order is reversed. Inversion may be a matter of grammar and *syntax*—reversing, for example, the normal order of subject and verb. (This is often done by Milton in *Paradise Lost* (e.g., "What in me is dark illumine"; "Man he made, and for him built magnificent this world"). Other forms of inversion as a matter of grammar and syntax include reversing the normal order of noun and adjective ("The sun shone bright along the boulevards wide, / Between the towers tall") or of adverb and verb ("softly flows the stream").

As a matter of poetic *meter* rather than syntax, inversion occurs when, for example, a *trochee* occurs in a line of *iambic* verse; in that *foot* the normal order of stressed and unstressed syllables is inverted. In this line, the fourth foot inverts the regular iambic meter: "When **spring-** / time **sings** / like **sum-** / mer, **bright** / **songs** of / my **love** / re- **turn**."

invitation poem: Genre of love poetry, identified by literary scholar Erik Gray, in which the beloved is invited to come with the lover to some other place—usually an idealized location in

i

the natural world. According to the conventions of the genre (which has its roots in the biblical Song of Songs), the attractions of the idealized natural place and those of the lover are often brought together; the former is often a poetic "stand-in" for the latter. Christopher Marlowe's "The Passionate Shepherd to his Love" (1599) is the best-known example of the genre in English literature of the *Renaissance*.

invocation: passage at the beginning of a literary work in which the author invokes the assistance and support of others—according to the conventions of *epic* poetry of the classical period, the support of one or more deities (most commonly, the *Muses*).

Irigaray, Luce: see *feminism / feminist criticism and theory / gender-based criticism and theory.*

Irish Literary Renaissance: period of remarkable literary activity and accomplishment by Irish writers in the late nineteenth and early twentieth centuries. The term is most commonly used in connection with the work of writers such as W.B. Yeats (1865-1939), Lady Gregory (1852-1932), J.M. Synge (1871-1909), and Sean O'Casey (1880-1964), who made strong efforts to revive interest in Irish traditions; during the same period a number of other writers of Irish background—among them Oscar Wilde (1854-1900) and James Joyce (1882-1941)—were making their own powerful impact on the literary world.

irony: the use of irony draws attention to a gap between what is said and what is meant, or what appears to be true and what is true. Types of irony include verbal irony (which includes, for example, *hyperbole*, *litotes*, and *sarcasm*), *dramatic irony*, and structural irony (in which the gap between what is "said" and meant is sustained throughout an entire piece, as when an author makes use of an unreliable narrator or speaker).

Iser, Wolfgang: see *implied reader*.

Italian sonnet: see *sonnet (Italian / Petrarchan)*.

Jacobean: from the period 1603-25, when James I was the English monarch (he was also James VI of Scotland). *Jacobus* is Latin for James.

James, William: see *stream of consciousness*.

Jesus Christ: see *mythopoeic theory and criticism*, *passion play*.

Jonson, Ben: see *masque*.

Joyce, James: see *epiphany*, *free indirect style / free indirect discourse*, *interior monologue*, *stream of consciousness*.

Jung, Carl: see *mythopoeic theory and criticism*, *psychoanalytic criticism*.

juvenilia: collective noun denoting the literary output of an author before he or she is deemed to have matured as a writer. The well-known juvenilia of Jane Austen (1775-1817), for example, consist of her writings from ages eleven to seventeen. An author's juvenilia need not always date from when he or she was a juvenile, however; the juvenilia of Philip Larkin (1922-85), for example, have often been taken to include poems he wrote in his late teens and early twenties, when he had still not developed a literary voice of his own.

Kandinsky, Wassily: see *expressionism / impressionism*.

Keats, John: see *elegy*, *feminine ending*, *Horatian ode*, *negative capability*.

kenning: a poetic expression in *Old English* in which two (usually concrete, compound) nouns are substituted for a noun used in everyday speech; e.g., "glory-father" for "god"; "building-mouth" for "door"; "sea-wood" for "ship"; "bone-house" for "body." Kennings have the effect of making descriptions more vivid; they may also act to subtly alter the ways in which we understand the meanings of a poem.

Kerouac, Jack: see *Beat Writing*.

King, Stephen: see *Gothic*.

Kirchner, Ernst Ludwig: see *expressionism / impressionism*.

kitsch: artistic or cultural artifacts that are valued for perceived qualities such as a tastelessness that is expressive of an earlier era, a comical shallowness, or an excessive striving to appeal to a mass audience at a low level of intellectual content. Classic examples include velvet images of Elvis Presley and plastic statuettes of Jesus intended for mounting on the dashboard of one's car.

Klages, Ludwig: see *logocentric*.

Kokoshka, Oskar: see *expressionism / impressionism*.

Kristeva, Julia: see *feminism / feminist criticism and theory / gender-based criticism and theory, psychoanalytic criticism*.

Lacan, Jacques: see *psychoanalytic criticism, structuralism / poststructuralism*.

lament: a poem that expresses profound regret or grief either because of a death, or because of the loss of a former, happier state.

language poetry: a movement that defies the usual lyric and narrative conventions of poetry, and that challenges the structures and codes of everyday language. It emerged primarily in America in the 1970s and 1980s; leading American language poets include Charles Bernstein (b. 1950) and Rae Armantrout (b. 1947). Often seen as both politically and aesthetically subversive, it has roots in the works of *modernist* writers such as Ezra Pound (1885-1972) and Gertrude Stein (1874-1946).

Larkin, Philip: see *juvenilia.*

Larsen, Nella: see *Harlem Renaissance.*

Latinate: in the context of English literature, the term "Latinate" may refer to poetry that frequently follows syntactic structures characteristic of Latin—notably, the inversion of the noun-verb sequence that is the most common ordering in English. (See *inversion* for examples from the poetry of John Milton.)

If an author's work is characterized by Latinate *diction*, it features nouns derived from Latin rather than from Anglo-Saxon (e.g., "donate" instead of "give"; "pernicious" instead of "evil"; "deceased" instead of "dead").

Lauretis, Teresa de: see *queer theory.*

lays: Celtic romantic tales in poetic form, often involving elements of the fantastic. In their twelfth-century form (best known to us through the *lais* of Marie de France) lays are typically less than 1,000 lines long and are written in rhyming couplets, with each line having eight syllables.

Leavis, F.R.: see *New Criticism.*

Leavitt, Sarah: see *graphic literature.*

leitmotif: recurring image or pattern of events in a literary work that helps to convey the work's theme. The German term *Leitmotiv* literally means "leading or guiding pattern"; it was first applied artistically as a descriptor of the musical patterns that suggest the themes of Richard Wagner's operas.

Lévi-Strauss, Claude: see *binary thinking, structuralism / poststructuralism.*

Lewis, Wyndham: see *futurism, Vorticism.*

life writing: an umbrella term used to refer to the genres of biography, memoir, autobiography, diaries, and journals—non-fictional writing that is based on the author's own lived experience or (in the case of biography) on the life of another person.

The line that separates fiction from non-fiction can be hard to determine, and this is often true in the case of life writing. No work that calls itself "life writing" can be the product of pure invention—if you make up the entire story, you are writing fiction—yet many authors of literary life writing consider it a legitimate practice to shape the presentation of events or characters in ways that deviate from the specifics of what actually happened. George Orwell (1903-50), one of the most highly acclaimed autobiographers of the twentieth century, is known to have done this frequently. So too, in the preface to one of the most influential autobiographical works of the recent decades, *Dreams from My Father* (1995), does Barack Obama candidly acknowledge that at least part of what he has written is, in some sense, fiction:

> Although much of this book is based on contemporaneous journals or the oral histories of my family, the dialogue is necessarily an approximation of what was actually said or relayed to me. For the sake of compression, some of the characters that appear are composites of people I've known, and some events appear out of precise chronology.

In other words, the writer has felt at liberty to sift and shape the material to give a personal view of what seems to him to be, in his words, "some granite slab of truth." Obama goes on to acknowledge the difficulty in naming this sort of writing: "Whatever the label that attaches to this book—autobiography, memoir, family history, or something else—what I've tried to do is write an honest account of a particular province of my life."

limerick: a fixed poetic form used for comic verse; a limerick is made up of five lines that combine *iambs* with *anapests*. The first, second, and fifth lines of a limerick each have three *feet*, the third and fourth lines two; the rhyme scheme is *aabba*. The form was popularized by Edward Lear in the mid-nineteenth century. Here is an example:

> A spritely young lad from Southend
> With far too much money to spend
> Bought far too much beer,
> Had far too much cheer,
> And ceased to be spritely. The end.

litotes: a *figure of speech* (a *trope*) in which a writer deliberately uses understatement to highlight the importance of an argument, or to convey an ironic attitude.

liturgical drama: drama based on, and/or incorporating text from, a liturgy—the text recited during religious services.

logocentric: a term first used in the 1920s by the German philosopher Ludwig Klages, and given wider currency by the French thinker Jacques Derrida in the 1960s and 1970s. If an approach (or a system) is logocentric, it tends to privilege the spoken over the written word, and also to presume that words correspond to some form of objective reality. In Derrida's view, the logocentric tendencies of Western culture have led Western thought to be overly concerned with concepts such as identity and, conversely, to pay insufficient attention to what Derrida called *différance*.

logos: along with *ethos* and *pathos*, one of the three categories of appeal that are set out in classical *rhetoric*. For Aristotle and other ancient Greek authorities, an appeal to logos was one based on reasoning, on logic. The term is now often used more broadly to refer to any appeal based on the ideas that are given expression in the words of a speech or a piece of writing.

London, Jack: see *animal studies*.

loose sentence: see *periodic sentence*.

Lowell, Robert: see *confessional poetry*.

Luther, Martin: see *humanism / Renaissance humanism*.

Lyly, John: see *euphuistic, mannerism*.

lyric: a poem, usually short, expressing an individual speaker's feelings or private thoughts. Originally a song performed with accompaniment on a lyre, the lyric poem is often noted for musicality of rhyme and rhythm. The lyric genre includes a variety of forms, including the *sonnet*, the *ode*, the *elegy*, the *madrigal*, the *aubade*, the *dramatic monologue*, and the *hymn*.

Macdonald, Ross: see *noir*.

MacEwen, Gwendolyn: see *mythopoeic theory and criticism*.

Macpherson, Jay: see *mythopoeic theory and criticism*.

madrigal: a *lyric* poem, usually short and focusing on *pastoral* or romantic themes. A madrigal is often set to music.

magic realism: a style of fiction in which miraculous or bizarre things often happen but are treated in a matter-of-fact fashion by the characters and/or the narrative voice. There is often an element of the absurd to magic realist narratives, and they tend not to have any strong plot structure generating expectations in the reader's mind. Authors associated with magic realism include Gabriel García Márquez (b. 1928), Jorge Luis Borges (1899-1986), and Salman Rushdie (b. 1947). See also *fantasy*.

malapropism: mistaken use of an inappropriate word for another word with a similar sound. The term derives from one Mrs. Malaprop (a character in Richard Brinsley Sheridan's eighteenth-century comedy *The Rivals*), who is given to making such mistakes. "Illiterate him ... from your memory," she advises another character at one point—meaning, of course, "Obliterate him ... from your memory."

Mallarmé, Stéphane: see *symbolist movement*.

Malory, Sir Thomas: see *Middle English, novel*.

mannerism: In the visual arts, Mannerism has a quite precise meaning; it names the stylized, elaborate, and often exaggerated painting style of such sixteenth-century painters as Rosso and Pontormo; as a period in Italian art; Mannerism follows the High Renaissance and precedes the Baroque. The term is used much more loosely (and usually with a lower-case "m") when it is applied to literature, to refer to various styles that in one way or another draw the reader's attention to the manner of presentation. The elaborate and highly stylized prose style of John Lyly's *Euphues* (1578-80; see also *euphuism*) has been described as mannerist, as has the poetic style of John Milton (1608-74), with its elevated *diction* and *Latinate* inversions.

Margalit, Avishai: see *Orientalism*.

marginalia: material written or printed in the margins of the pages in a book or manuscript. An example is the 1817 version of the long poem "The Rime of the Ancient Mariner" by Samuel

Taylor Coleridge (who invented the term "marginalia"), which includes marginal annotations throughout.

Marie de France: see *feminism / feminist criticism and theory / gender-based criticism and theory, lays.*

Marlowe, Christopher: see *invitation poem.*

Marvell, Andrew: see *carpe diem, metaphysical poets.*

Marx, Karl: see *cultural materialism / cultural studies, historicism / new historicism, Marxist theory and criticism.*

Marxist theory and criticism: literary theory and criticism stemming from or inspired by the work of Karl Marx (1818-83) and his followers. Marx and his colleague Friedrich Engels (1820-95) gave shape to their philosophy in mid-nineteenth-century England, at a time when the benefits of industrialization were concentrated very much in the hands of the capitalists, and the workers who provided the labor (as well as those dependent on the workers) received far less than their due. Marx and Engels argued that these were not temporary conditions unique to Britain at that time, but rather conditions fundamental to the operation of the capitalist system. Ideas central to Marxism include a conviction that private ownership of property and of "the means of production" is inimical to the well-being of humans; a belief in the importance of work and, accompanying that belief, a conviction that some degree of control over the products of one's labor is essential to human flourishing; a belief that capitalism tends to alienate workers from the products of their own labor—and in turn to alienate them from an important part of their own natures; an acknowledgment of the importance of ideology to culture—and an awareness that people cannot avoid having their world outlook heavily (and often unconsciously) colored

m

by the dominant ideology of the society in which they are raised; a conviction that capitalism holds within it forces that are inherently oppressive for workers—but that it also holds within it the seeds of its own destruction; a strong sense that progress is to be achieved through the opposition of (largely class-based) forces, leading to revolution and, eventually, to a classless society; a belief that there is a historical inevitability to the movement of the forces that must be involved in these developments; a conviction that, in general, change is a product of socio-economic forces—especially of economic ones—and that the power of individuals to shape change is severely limited; and a belief that, in general, the collective rather than the individual is deserving of emphasis.

As is the case with so-called "*Freudian*" approaches to literature, it is rare that literary critics or theorists broadly described as having adopted "Marxist approaches" to literature are doctrinaire followers of a set of nineteenth-century ideas. What is denoted through the use of terms such as "Freudian" or "Marxist" in this context is rather the general tenor of the approach taken. Approaches to literature that are influenced by the tradition of Marxist thought tend to emphasize the collective over the individual; tend when considering the forces that have shaped a work's creation to place more emphasis on the society out of which that work emerged than they do on the author as an individual; tend to de-emphasize the characters of a work as unique individuals, and instead to consider how those characters reflect the socio-economic forces of their society and their era; and tend to pay substantial attention to the ways in which literary works may embody the assumptions and the contradictions of the socio-economic systems out of which they have emerged.

Marxist ideas had an important direct influence on literature, especially in the 1930s, the height of Socialist realism (a movement that glorified the struggle of the working classes in painting and sculpture, but also in literary works such as Mikhail Sholokhov's *And Quiet Flows the Don* [1928-40]), and also the decade during which Bertolt Brecht gave expression to theories concerning the *alienation effect* in a series of influential plays.

Marxist theoretical and critical approaches have some affinity with certain other ways of approaching literary theory and criticism—notably *cultural materialism* and *new historicism*. Among the most important critics and theorists who have been influenced by Marxism are Walter Benjamin (1892-1940), Raymond Williams (1921-88), Fredric Jameson (b. 1934), and, in his early work, Terry Eagleton (b. 1943).

masculine ending: in *accentual-syllabic* poetry, the end of a metrical line that finishes with a stressed syllable; an alternative term is "hard landing." Since *iambic* verse is the most common metrical form in English, most lines of accentual-syllabic verse in English end with a hard landing.

masculine rhyme: rhyme involving the stressed, final syllables of lines of poetry; an alternative term is "one-syllable rhyme." In contrast, feminine rhyme (for which the alternative term is *double rhyme*) involves both a stressed syllable and the following, unstressed syllable. The lines of the first of the following examples end in a one-syllable rhyme ("sky" / "die"); the lines of the second example end in a double rhyme ("fly-ing" / "dy-ing"):

> The planets, moons, and stars that fill the sky
> Seem bright as ever always; all must die.

> Planets, moons, and stars, so brightly flying,
> Are all of them, like all we know, always slowly dying.

masque: an early-modern genre of court entertainment featuring acting, songs, dances, elaborate masks and costumes, and innovative set machinery, all of which combined to create an impressive—and expensive—spectacle. A typical masque had an allegorical plot, often borrowed from mythology, which could be interpreted in praise of the production's royal patrons. Members of the noble class performed in the masque, and their casting contributed to its allegorical themes. The playwright and poet Ben Jonson (1572-1637) wrote the best-known examples of the genre in English; he was also the first to include an "antimasque," a short, comic performance with strong disorderly elements, in contrast to the refinement of the masque itself.

McCarthy, Cormac: see *speculative fiction*.

McCrae, John: see *rondeau*.

Mellor, Anne K.: see *feminism / feminist criticism and theory / gender-based criticism and theory*.

melodrama: originally a term used to describe nineteenth-century plays featuring sensational story lines and a crude separation of characters into moral categories, with the pure and virtuous pitted against evil villains. Early melodramas employed background music throughout the action of the play as a means of heightening the emotional response of the audience. By extension, certain sorts of prose fictions or poems are often described as having melodramatic elements.

Melville, Herman: see *Transcendentalism*.

metafiction: fiction that calls attention to itself as fiction, often in an effort to explore the relationships between fiction and reality. Metafictional situations occur, for example, when the writing refers to the act of reading or writing, when an author seems to insert himself or herself into the story as a character, or when an author seems to address the reader directly or interrupt the narrative.

metaphor: a *figure of speech* (in this case, a *trope*) in which a comparison is made or identity is asserted between two unrelated things or actions without the use of "like" or "as." The primary subject is known as the "tenor"; to illuminate its nature, the writer links it to wholly different images, ideas, or actions referred to as the "vehicle." Unlike a *simile*, which is a direct comparison of two things, a metaphor "fuses" the separate qualities of two things, creating a new idea. For example, Shakespeare's "Let slip the dogs of war" is a metaphorical statement. The tenor, or primary subject, is "war"; the vehicle of the metaphor is the image of hunting dogs released from their leash. The line fuses the idea of war with the qualities of ravening bloodlust associated with hunting dogs.

metaphysical poets: a group of seventeenth-century English poets (notably John Donne, Abraham Cowley, Andrew Marvell, and George Herbert) who employed unusual, difficult *imagery* and *conceits* in order to develop intellectual and religious themes. The term was first applied to these writers to mark as far-fetched their use of philosophical and scientific ideas in a poetic context. Though "metaphysical poets" is still widely used as a term of convenience, many literary historians now regard it as one that may tend to flatten the variety of approaches taken by these poets—and thereby to oversimplify.

metatheater: a term coined by the critic Lionel Abel (1910-2001) to describe theater that draws attention to the fact that it is a fictional performance. Common metatheatrical techniques include the "play within a play" (in *Hamlet*, for example, Hamlet enlists actors to perform a play duplicating aspects of his father's murder); *parody* that mocks theatrical conventions; and reference to the performance's actors (as opposed to characters) or its audience. Such techniques can disrupt the realism of a play, and can raise questions about the nature of theater, the relationship between theater and real life, and the ways in which real life resembles theatrical performance. See also *alienation effect*, *metafiction*.

meter: the pattern of stresses, syllables, and pauses that constitutes the regular rhythm of a line of verse. The meter of a poem written in the English *accentual-syllabic* tradition is determined by identifying the stressed and unstressed syllables in a line of verse, and grouping them into recurring units known as *feet*. See *accent*, *accentual-syllabic*, *caesura*, *elision*, and *scansion*. For some of the better-known meters, see *anapest*, *dactyl*, *iamb*, *spondee*, and *trochee*. For lengths of metrical lines, see *monometer*, *dimeter*, *trimeter*, *tetrameter*, *pentameter*, and *hexameter*.

metonymy: a *figure of speech* (a *trope*), meaning "change of name," in which a writer refers to an object or idea by substituting the name of another object or idea closely associated with it: for example, the substitution of "crown" for monarchy, "the press" for journalism, or "the pen" for writing. *Synecdoche* is a kind of metonymy.

Middle English: the form(s) of English in use from c. 1100 to c. 1450. The language of Anglo-Saxon England in the period preceding Middle English is known as *Old English*. Considerably different both in sound and in structure from later varieties of English, Old English also used some letters not found in the Roman alphabet, including thorn (þ) and eth (ð), both of which signified the sound represented nowadays by the sequence "th"; thorn survived well into Middle English, where it gradually came to be written much like the letter y (giving rise to the common misreading of "ye" for "the" in faux-antique signs like "ye olde shoppe"). In the two or three centuries following the Norman

m

conquest of 1066, English absorbed a huge number of French words (which led to the use of another new letter, yogh: ȝ, and to the use of the letters j and q), as well as some of the structural elements of the French language; many Old English words became obsolete, but many others continued to exist alongside their French counterparts, enriching the English lexicon. The inflected endings of many Old English words were simplified or dropped, and there began to be more distinctions made through the sounds of vowels. And, whereas the dialect known as West Saxon had predominated in Old English, there was considerably more regional variation in the various forms of Middle English.

Middle English is distinguished from Modern English in large part by pronunciation. As in Old English, all consonants are sounded, including those in combinations such as kn, gn, lk, and wr that have become largely or entirely silent in Modern English. The word "knight," for example, is pronounced something like "k-neecht." The pronunciation of vowels has changed even more dramatically. Before the so-called "Great Vowel Shift" that began in the early fifteenth century, the vowel sound in "made" was pronounced in much the same way as we now pronounce the vowel sound in "mad" or "sad," the vowel sound in "sweet" was pronounced as we now pronounce the vowel sound in "mate" or "fate," and the vowel sound in "food" and "good" was pronounced as we now pronounce the vowel sound in "rowed" or "snowed." Many previously multi-syllabic words (e.g., liv-es, hel-ped) came to be pronounced as one syllable. Word order in Middle English is often substantially different from modern practice; adjectives often followed nouns, for example, as is the practice in French; thus Malory refers to the "table round" of King Arthur.

Midgley, Mary: see *animal studies*.

Mill, John Stuart: see *novel*.

Miller, Arthur: see *problem play*.

Milton, John: see *catachresis, elegy, epic, hyperbole, inversion, Latinate, mannerism, oxymoron, pastoral elegy, sonnet (Miltonic)*.

Miltonic sonnet: see *sonnet (Miltonic)*.

mimesis: from the Greek word meaning "to imitate." In literature, "mimesis" is the portrayal of reality. The concept was of fundamental importance to ancient Greek theory and was introduced by Plato, who argued that art was a reflection of the observed world. Aristotle understood mimesis more broadly as drawing on and interpreting aspects of the real world *not* in order to imitate reality directly but in order to portray some sort of truth about how the world is—and especially how human beings are—or should be. The concept of mimesis has retained importance throughout the history of literary criticism and has been frequently reinterpreted as a way of considering the nature of literature, its purpose and value, and its relationship to reality.

miracle play: a term once widely applied to certain forms of medieval religious drama; it is now widely regarded as unhelpful. See *biblical plays*.

mise en scène: French expression, literally meaning "the putting on stage," which has been adopted in other languages to describe the sum total of creative choices made in the staging of a play. In film the term is used in similar fashion to refer to everything that goes into the arrangement of the action. (It does not, however, include elements such as the camerawork, or the process of editing the film.)

mixed metaphor: *metaphor* in which two (or more) logically incompatible likenesses are mixed up with each other (e.g., "if we bite the bullet we will have to be careful not to throw the baby out with the bathwater").

mock-heroic: a style applying the elevated *diction* and vocabulary of *epic* poetry to low or ridiculous subjects. An example is Alexander Pope's *The Rape of the Lock* (1712).

Modern English: the form(s) of the English language in use from the sixteenth century onwards. See also *Middle English*.

modernism: an umbrella term used to describe a wide range of inter-connected intellectual and aesthetic developments of the first half of the twentieth century that occurred in France, Italy, the United States, Britain, and other areas. Modernists tended to shun the linear, the decorative, and the sentimental, and to present reality as fractured into its component pieces. This meant abandoning many of the approaches we tend to associate with realistic literature—such as a single point of view or a single, unbroken narrative—but it was often suggested that the fractured forms of modernism might represent the world as humans *perceive* it more realistically than other, seemingly more "realistic" forms of representation.

Virginia Woolf wrote in a frequently quoted essay that "on or about December 1910 human character changed." Woolf saw that date as marking the moment at which writers began smashing literary conventions in an effort to represent the complexity of human experience through "the spasmodic, the obscure, the fragmentary." At the same moment, painting and sculpture were breaking visual reality into fragments to express the reality of fragmented experience—or indeed to express the reality of what increasingly seemed a fragmented world. Such is now a conventional account of the birth of modernism.

There was, of course, a mock-precision in Woolf's dating, but many others have linked the birth of Modernism to developments that occurred at *about* this time: in painting, the development of Cubism by Pablo Picasso and Georges Braque; in music, the development of strikingly discordant styles such as that of Stravinsky's *The Rite of Spring*; in poetry, the development of *Imagism* and its offshoots by Ezra Pound, H.D. and, a few years later, T.S. Eliot; and in fiction, the development by Dorothy Richardson, James Joyce, Virginia Woolf, and others of *stream of consciousness* techniques of narration. Arguably, though, the birth of modernism can be traced to developments that occurred in France considerably earlier—developments such as the *symbolist* movement of the late nineteenth century.

molossus: poetic *foot* composed of three stressed syllables.

monodrama: this term, which originated in the eighteenth century, has often been used to describe dramatic works in which one character engages in an extended monologue; Samuel Beckett's *Krapp's Last Tape* (1958), a play in which the entire action consists of the protagonist speaking into a tape recorder, is a notable twentieth-century example. Perhaps the best-known use of the term, however, is by Tennyson, who uses it in the title of his long 1856 poem *Maud; A Monodrama*; his use of the term to refer to a long poem composed of a series of dramatic monologues is unique.

monologue: words spoken by a character to himself or herself, or to an audience directly.

monometer: a line containing one metrical *foot*.

Montaigne, Michel de: see *essay*.

mood: this term can describe the writer's attitude, implied or expressed, toward the subject (see *tone*); or it may refer to the atmosphere that a writer creates in a passage of description or narration.

More, Thomas: see *humanism / Renaissance humanism, Utopian literature.*

Morton, Jelly Roll: see *Harlem Renaissance.*

motif: an idea, image, action, or plot element that recurs throughout a literary work, creating new levels of meaning and strengthening structural coherence. The term is taken from music, where it describes recurring melodies or themes. See also *leitmotif, theme.*

motivations: the forces that seem to cause characters to act, or reasons why characters do what they do.

Munch, Edvard: see *expressionism / impressionism.*

muse: in Greek mythology, one of the daughters of Zeus and Mnemosyne; together the Muses are the goddesses of artistic inspiration. By extension, a writer may refer to his or her "muse," meaning his or her source of inspiration.

mystery play: a term once widely applied to certain forms of medieval religious drama; it is now widely regarded as unhelpful. See *biblical plays.*

mythopoeic theory and criticism: theory and criticism based on the underlying notion that, in the words of Northrop Frye, "the typical forms of myth become the conventions and genres of literature." Through an understanding of myth, in other words, one may achieve a deeper understanding of literature.

Substantial interest in myth among literary scholars developed in the nineteenth and early twentieth centuries; the great landmark of scholarship of this era was James Frazer's *The Golden Bough: A Study in Magic and Religion* (1890-1915), which treated the stories of mythology and those of religion in much the same fashion (Frazer's inclusion of the story of Jesus along with the myths of other cultures was highly controversial at the time), and which saw literary analysis and anthropological analysis as going hand in hand. Frazer's work exerted very considerable influence on literary figures (notably T.S. Eliot and Robert Graves) as well as on generations of scholars.

In the early twentieth century the psychiatrist and psycho-analytic theorist Carl Jung developed his own theory as to the elemental psychic components of human experience, which he called *archetypes*. According to Jung, archetypal figures such as the wise old woman and the trickster—figures often found in mythology—are part of the collective unconscious of all humans. Jungian archetypes have remained frequent reference points for literary critics and theorists—perhaps none more so than the shadow, an archetype that may stand for the unconscious self.

Frye (1912-91) was one of the leading lights of mid-twenti-eth-century literary theory and criticism. Frye sought patterns of knowledge that were held in common among myths and works of literature. His approach focused on the body of literature rather than on theories as to the collective unconscious; rather than regarding literature primarily as a way of structuring ideas, or as a set of aesthetic objects to be appreciated and evaluated, he saw literature largely in terms of the archetypal patterns in its narratives. But Frye was not focused exclusively on the connec-tions between myth and literature; far from it. His *Anatomy of Criticism* (1957) advanced what he saw as a systematic approach that would establish literary criticism as an academic discipline akin to those in the sciences. Both in literature and in literary criticism, he distinguished between centripetal movement (mov-ing inward, and focused on textual structure), and centrifugal (moving outward, aiming toward an understanding that extends from the text to society at large).

n

Frye taught at the University of Toronto for many decades, and his influence on Canadian literature and criticism was particularly strong. It has often been suggested that several of the leading figures of Canadian literature from the mid-1950s through to the mid-1970s—among them James Reaney (1926-2008), Jay Macpherson (1931-2012), Gwendolyn MacEwen (1941-87), and Margaret Atwood (b. 1939)—aimed in their literary work of this period to give expression to the theoretical and critical notions of Frye. (Atwood's own influential work of literary criticism from this period, *Survival*, shares some of the ideas about the mythic background to Canadian literature that Frye advances in his *The Bush Garden*.)

Frye's work was enormously influential throughout much of the English-speaking world in the 1970s and 1980s; since then his star has waned somewhat, but the mythopoeic approach remains common currency, especially in discussions of the literature of folk and fairy tales, of J.R.R. Tolkien and other authors of *fantasy* literature, and of *science fiction* and *speculative fiction*.

narration: the process of storytelling.

narrative perspective: in fiction, the point of view from which the story is narrated. A first-person narrative is recounted using "I" and "me," whereas a third-person narrative is recounted using "he," "she," "they," and so on. When a narrative is written in the third person and the narrative voice evidently "knows" all that is being done and thought, the story is typically described as being recounted by an "omniscient narrator." (Second-person narratives, in which the narrative is recounted using "you," are very rare.)

narratology / narrative theory: a branch of literary criticism and theory devoted to the analysis of narrative structure. One might expect that such a field would devote a good deal of time to analyzing subjects such as the roles that exposition and direct presentation may play in the development of narratives; the ways in which different approaches to plotting may build expectation; the issue of how different approaches to pacing may affect perceptions of character; or the effect of taking different approaches to beginning the story *in medias res* (rather than at the beginning). For whatever reason, however, these down-to-earth aspects of narrative have received little attention from literary critics and theorists; figures of other eras—from Aristotle to Gustav Freytag to William Archer—remain among the most helpful reference points.

Narratology, on the other hand, has developed as a subdiscipline of literary theory. It has been highly conceptual, often driven toward theoretical generalization, and often characterized by an urge to locate irreducible elements of narrative, the latter stemming in large part from the work of the *Russian formalist* Vladimir Propp (1895-1970), whose studies of the narrative elements of folk tales have been extremely influential. Narratology has been substantially informed by *structuralism*, *hermeneutics*, *semiotics*, and *discourse analysis*. Among the most influential figures in narratology have been Gérard Genette (b. 1930), whose *Narrative Discourse: An Essay in Method* appeared in 1980, and Paul Ricœur (1913-2005), whose three-volume *Time and Narrative* appeared in 1985.

narrator: the voice (or voices) telling the story. The narrator is distinct from both the author (a real, historical person) and the implied author (whom the reader imagines the author to be). Narrators can be distinguished according to the degree to which they share the reality of the other characters in the story and the extent to which they participate in the action; how much information they are privy to (and how much of that information

n

they are willing to share with the reader); and whether or not they are perceived by the reader as reliable or unreliable sources of information. See also *narrative perspective*.

Nashe, Thomas: see *novel*.

naturalism: movement aiming to represent the human world—including its less appealing aspects—directly and frankly in literature and the other arts. See also *realism*.

near rhyme: see *rhyme*.

Neely, Carol Thomas: see *feminism / feminist criticism and theory / gender-based criticism and theory*.

negative capability: the notion that in the creative process it may be unhelpful to look for positive certainty or to aim to achieve full explanations. The concept comes from a December 1817 letter by the poet John Keats to his brothers George and Thomas: "it struck me what quality went to form a Man of Achievement, especially in Literature, and which Shakespeare possessed so enormously—I mean Negative Capability, that is, when a man is capable of being in uncertainties, mysteries, doubts, without any irritable reaching after fact and reason." Keats opines that a poet should be capable of being "content with half-knowledge," but he then suggests that the concept of negative capability should itself perhaps not be pursued too far: "This pursued through volumes would perhaps take us no further than this, that with a great poet the sense of Beauty overcomes every other consideration, or rather obliterates all consideration."

nemesis: in Greek mythology, a spirit who brought divine retribution against those with excessive pride or ambition. By extension, a character's nemesis is the thing that brings about his or her downfall.

neoclassical dramaturgy: the principles, rules and *conventions* of writing plays according to the precepts and ideals of *neoclassicism*. Often based on the so-called *unities* of time, place, and action.

neoclassicism: literally the "new classicism," the aesthetic style that dominated high culture in Europe throughout the seventeenth and eighteenth centuries, and in some places into the nineteenth. Its subject matter was often taken from Greek and Roman myth and history; in style, it valued order, reason, clarity, and moderation.

Neo-Platonism: In the history of philosophy, "Neo-Platonism" is the name that has been applied since the nineteenth century to a school of thought originating with Plotinus (c. 204-70 CE) and other thinkers who regarded themselves as followers of Plato, the fourth-century BCE Greek philosopher. Central to Neo-Platonic thought is an often semi-mystical emphasis on the One, an ideal form to which all souls (and, in some variations, all things) aspire.

In the history of English literature, the revivals of Neo-Platonism (first in the sixteenth and seventeenth centuries and then in the late eighteenth century and the first half of the nineteenth) are of greater importance than its third-century roots. The *Renaissance* revival of Neo-Platonism began in Italy (led by Marsilio Ficino, 1433-99); elements of Renaissance Neo-Platonism may be found in the work of several English *metaphysical poets*. During the *Romantic* era, Neo-Platonist ideas influenced such continental writers as Johann Wolfgang von Goethe (1749-1832) and Rainer Maria Rilke (1875-1926), as well as the English Romantic poets William Wordsworth (1770-1850) and Percy Bysshe Shelley (1792-1822); later in the nineteenth century they also influenced several major figures in American literature—notably

Ralph Waldo Emerson (1803-82). See also *humanism / Renaissance humanism*.

n

New Criticism: an umbrella term for a variety of more-or-less *formalist* approaches to literary criticism that flourished between c. 1920 and the 1960s. The term was coined in 1941 by John Crowe Ransom to refer to literary criticism that was felt to be more precise and scientific than the criticism of late-nineteenth and early-twentieth-century figures such as Walter Pater and Sir Arthur Quiller-Couch. The mainstream of that body of criticism had often been impressionistic in character; had often brought biographical information to bear on discussions of literary texts; had focused extensively on discussions of individual characters (perhaps most notably, the characters of Shakespeare's plays), often in a tone that seemed to treat them as if they were real human beings; and had often aimed as much at fostering appreciation of literary works as it had at analyzing them. By contrast, New Critics tended to eschew the biographical; tended as well to eschew discussions of historical context or of ideology, preferring to analyze literary works in an ahistorical, apolitical fashion; emphasized *close reading* of the text; regarded *ambiguity* in literary texts as a particularly fruitful area for critical analysis; paid more attention to poetry than to other genres; and paid more attention to *imagery* and to *metaphor* than to other formal aspects of poetry (*meter*, for example, or *rhyme*). Cleanth Brooks's highly influential *The Well-Wrought Urn: Studies in the Structure of Poetry* (1947) is a paradigmatic work of New Criticism—expressive of all the above-mentioned tendencies. In addition to Ransom (1888-1974) and Brooks (1906-94), figures central to the New Criticism include William K. Wimsatt (b. 1941) and Monroe Beardsley (1915-85), who often published together; Allen Tate (1899-1979); and William Empson (1906-84).

Though subsequent discussions have often implied that the New Critics were a more-or-less homogenous group, in fact they did not form anything like a unified movement. T.S. Eliot (1888-1965), for example, who is often mentioned in discussions of New Criticism, was frequently impressionistic in his literary criticism and was very much alive to the importance of historical context. I.A. Richards (1893-1979), who did indeed attempt to be precise and scientific in his literary analyses, was also acutely aware of the importance of ideology in shaping literary work. F.R. Leavis (1895-1978), another who is sometimes associated with the New Critics, no doubt in large part for the acuteness of some of his observations on Victorian and modernist poetry, was always more interested in literary texts as part of a larger cultural (and moral) fabric than he was in isolating their formal, aesthetic qualities.

new formalism: among poets, new formalism is a movement originating in the late twentieth century that has endeavored to renew interest in verse written in traditional *accentual-syllabic meter*, in verse written in *fixed forms* (the *sonnet*, the *villanelle*, etc.), and in rhymed verse. The movement is centered in the United States, where writing in traditional forms became far rarer from the 1960s onwards than it was in Britain.

In the world of literary studies, the term has been used to refer to the increased interest among a variety of late-twentieth- and early-twenty-first-century scholars in matters relating to literary form (in the formal qualities of eighteenth- and nineteenth-century literature of sentiment, in nineteenth-century *prosody*, in the history of *free indirect discourse*—to pick only three examples). In contrast to some earlier sorts of *formalism* (notably, that of the *New Critics* of the mid-twentieth century) the new formalism is usually interested in drawing connections between the formal

n

qualities of literary works and the context of the historical and ideological circumstances out of which they emerged.

new historicism: See *historicism*.

New Woman literature: literature of the late nineteenth and early twentieth centuries pertaining to the so-called New Woman—young, politically and socially progressive, and prepared to challenge the era's conventions of feminine style by wearing trousers, smoking cigars, and riding bicycles. The category of New Woman literature includes both imaginative works by writers such as Sarah Grand (1854-1943) that aimed to criticize social strictures and promote the New Woman as an ideal, and works by writers such as Grant Allen (1848-99) that aimed to ridicule the movement.

Newton, Judith: see *feminism / feminist criticism and theory / gender-based criticism and theory*.

Nietzsche, Friedrich: see *Apollonian*.

noir: originally a term relating to film, denoting a subgenre of 1940s-1950s black-and-white pictures dealing largely with crime and/or with seamy aspects of urban life. Works in the film noir tradition often turn on characters' powerful sexual *motivations*; are often somewhat *melodramatic* in tone; are often expressive of a cynical or pessimistic view of human nature; and tend to be visually as well as thematically dark in tone—characterized by shadows and strong contrasts between light and dark (hence the "noir"—French for "black"). The term is now often also used to refer to literary work, and in particular to works of fiction—by such authors as James Cain (1892-1977), Raymond Chandler (1888-1959), Dashiell Hammett (1894-1961), and Ross Macdonald (1915-83)—on which some of the great works of film noir were based.

nonsense verse: light, humorous poetry that contradicts logic, plays with the absurd, and invents words for amusing effects. Lewis Carroll (1832-98) is one of the best-known practitioners of nonsense verse.

n

novel: an extended work of prose fiction. It is impossible to be precise as to how "extended" a work of fiction must be to qualify as a novel (as opposed to a short story or a novella). Some have suggested as a rough guideline that works of prose fiction shorter than about 20,000 words should be classed as novellas (or long short stories).

Ironically, the word "novel" in this sense in English derives from the Italian *novella* ("little new thing")—a word used in the fourteenth century to denote not a long narrative but a short tale, of the sort found in Boccaccio's *Decameron* (a form of fiction, in other words, that would now be considered far too brief to qualify as a novel).

Another oft-discussed issue is the degree to which a novel is to be distinguished from a prose *romance*. (The word for novel in French—*roman*—and in several other languages has the same root as our "romance.") Though the history of the novel in English is said by many to begin with Aphra Behn and Daniel Defoe in the late seventeenth and early eighteenth centuries, others point to its roots in fifteenth- and sixteenth-century prose romances such as Philip Sidney's *Arcadia* and Sir Thomas Malory's *Le Morte Darthur*—and in works of Elizabethan popular prose fiction that cannot readily be classed as romances (Thomas Deloney's *Jack of Newbury*, for example, or Thomas Nashe's *The Unfortunate Traveller*).

Above all, it is essential to keep in mind that a novel is a work of prose fiction—not any original work. Non-fiction works are never novels. John Stuart Mill's *On Liberty* (1859) is a work of philosophy and political theory, not a novel; George Orwell's

Homage to Catalonia (1938) is a memoir and historical-political study, not a novel; Virginia Woolf's *A Room of One's Own* (1929) may be described as a series of *essays*, as a work of personal reflection, as a study of history and of politics, as a groundbreaking work of *feminist* analysis; it may not be described as a novel, for it is not fiction; it is not made up. Nor are *Beowulf* or Elizabeth Barrett Browning's *Aurora Leigh* novels; these are works of fiction, but they are works of poetry, not of prose.

novella: see *novel*.

Nuttall, A.D.: see *Theory*.

Obama, Barack: see *life writing*, *parallelism*.

oblique rhyme: see *rhyme*.

O'Casey, Sean: see *Irish Literary Renaissance*.

occasional verse: verse written to mark an occasion. Often (though not always), occasional verse may be commissioned or have some official status; as Poet Laureate, for example, Carol Ann Duffy wrote "Rings" to officially commemorate the 2011 marriage of Prince William and Kate Middleton.

O'Connor, Flannery: see *foreshadowing*, *grotesque*.

octave: also known as an "octet," the first eight lines in a Petrarchan *sonnet*, rhyming *abbaabba*. See also *sestet* and *sonnet (Petrarchan)*.

octavo: book format in which sheets of paper are folded to produce eight leaves; on each leaf are two pages, so the gathered sections (or signatures) of an octavo book are made up of 16 pages each. The size of octavo-format books varies depending on the size of the sheets used; common sizes range from 5x7 inches to 6x9 inches.

octosyllabic: a line of poetry with eight syllables, as in *iambic tetrameter*.

ode: originally a classical poetic form, used by the Greeks and Romans to convey serious themes. English poetry has evolved three main forms of ode: the Pindaric (imitative of the odes of the fifth-century BCE Greek poet Pindar); the *Horatian* (modeled on the work of the first-century BCE Roman writer Horace); and the irregular ode. The Pindaric ode has a tripartite structure of *strophe*, *antistrophe*, and *epode* (meaning "turn," "counterturn," and "stand"), modeled on the songs and movements of the chorus in Greek drama. The Horatian ode is more personal, reflective, and literary, and employs a pattern of repeated stanzas. The irregular ode, as its name implies, avoids a recurrent stanza pattern, and is sometimes irregular in line length also (an example is Wordsworth's 1804 poem "Ode: Intimations of Immortality").

Old English: the form of English in use before the late eleventh century. See also *Middle English*.

Olson, Charles: see *Black Mountain School*.

omniscient narrator: see *narrative perspective*.

O'Neill, Eugene: see *expressionism / impressionism*.

Ong, Walter: see *oral tradition*, *print culture / history of the book*.

onomatopoeia: a *figure of speech* (a scheme) in which a word "imitates" a sound, or in which the sound of a word seems to reflect its meaning.

oral tradition: literary, historical, mythological, or other material of cultural value that is passed on orally, often over many generations. Key areas of study of oral tradition have included the

O

Homeric narratives; early *Old English* and Old Norse narrative poetry; the early transmission of English *ballads*; the development of folk and fairy tales in Europe; and the transmission of myths and other narratives among the native peoples of North America. The effects of literacy on cognition and on culture have also been the focus of substantial interest; among the most important critics and theorists in this area are Walter Ong (1912-2003) and John Miles Foley (1947-2012).

orchestra: literally, "the dancing place." In ancient Greek drama, the orchestra was the lower, flat, circular surface-area of the outdoor theater where the *chorus* danced and sang.

Orientalism: the view that the cultures of Asia and the Middle East share a variety of fundamental characteristics, and that it is thus appropriate to broadly class them together—and to broadly contrast the characteristics of those societies with those presumed to be fundamental to Western (or "Occidental") societies. In his enormously influential 1978 book *Orientalism*, Edward Said traced the tendency in Western societies to group widely divergent cultures into binary categories in this way, and found connections between the ways in which Westerners had romanticized the "mysterious East" and the ways in which they had demonized it. Several scholars—Ian Buruma (b. 1951) and Avishai Margalit (b. 1939) most prominent among them—have argued that a similar phenomenon, Occidentalism, has operated in the other direction. See also *essentialism*.

Orwell, George: see *life writing, novel, speculative fiction*.

ottava rima: an eight-line stanza, usually in *iambic pentameter*, with the rhyme scheme *abababcc*. For an example, see Byron's *Don Juan* (1819-24), or Yeats's "Sailing to Byzantium" (1928).

Ovid: see *humanism / Renaissance humanism*.

oxymoron: a *figure of speech* (a *trope*) in which two words whose meanings seem contradictory are placed together; a paradox: for example, the phrase "darkness visible," from Milton's *Paradise Lost* (1667).

Ozeki, Ruth: see *animal studies*.

paean: a triumphant, celebratory song, often associated with a military victory.

Page, P.K.: see *glosa*.

palimpsest: a page that is almost clean after having had a previous text washed or scraped off, but on which traces remain of the work previously inscribed. It was common practice to re-use manuscripts in this way in classical Greece and Rome, and throughout much of the Middle Ages in Europe. As a result, a number of texts are known to us only as palimpsests—faintly legible remains. A notable example recently uncovered is the work of the third-century BCE Greek mathematician Archimedes, the sole surviving copy of which had been overwritten with a prayer book in the thirteenth century.

palindrome: a word or phrase that remains the same whether one reads it forwards or backwards. The word "radar" is a palindrome—as is the phrase "never odd or even."

pantoum: a poem in linked *quatrains* that rhyme *abab*. The second and fourth lines of one stanza are repeated as the first and third lines of the stanza that follows. In the final stanza the pattern is reversed: the second line repeats the third line of the first stanza, and the fourth and final line repeats the first line of the first stanza.

parable: a short story told to illustrate a moral principle. It differs from *allegory* in being shorter and simpler: parables do not generally function on two levels simultaneously.

parallelism: the combining of words, phrases, etc. so as to create structural parallels. Parallelism may take many forms. When Abraham Lincoln (1809-65) spoke of "government of the people, by the people, for the people," he was using parallelism in successive phrases. When Elizabeth Cady Stanton (1815-1902) said of the right of women to vote, "Have it, we must. Use it, we will," she was using parallelism in successive sentences. When Barack Obama ended each of several paragraphs near the end of his 2008 election-night speech with the words "Yes, we can," he was using parallelism in successive paragraphs. And when the writers of this glossary structured this entry, they too were using parallelism.

paraphrase: the expression of ideas using words substantially different from those in which they have already been expressed. Note that a paraphrase need not be shorter than the original; it need not involve summary.

parody: a close, usually mocking imitation of a particular literary work, or of the well-known style of a particular author, in order to expose or magnify weaknesses. Parody is a form of *satire*—that is, humor that may ridicule and scorn its object.

paronomasia: see *pun*.

partial rhyme: see *rhyme*.

passion play: a play depicting the sufferings ("passion") of Jesus Christ. Performances of such plays are often a part of Roman Catholic tradition during Lent—the season that leads up to Good Friday (the commemoration of Christ's crucifixion) and Easter Sunday (the celebration of his resurrection and ascent to heaven, three days after he was killed).

pastiche: a discourse that borrows or imitates other writers' characters, forms, style, or ideas. Unlike a *parody*, a pastiche is usually intended as a compliment to the original writer or writers.

pastoral: in general, pertaining to country life; in prose, drama, and poetry, a stylized type of writing that idealizes the lives and innocence of country people, particularly shepherds and shepherdesses. See also *eclogue*, *georgic*, and *idyll*.

pastoral elegy: a poem in which the poet uses the *pastoral* style to lament the death of a friend, usually represented as a shepherd. Milton's "Lycidas" (1637) provides a good example of the form, including its use of such *conventions* as an invocation of the *muse* and a procession of mourners.

Pater, Walter: see *New Criticism*.

pathetic fallacy: a form of *personification* in which inanimate objects are given human emotions: for example, rain clouds "weeping." The word "fallacy" in this connection is intended to suggest the distortion of reality or the false emotion that may result from an exaggerated use of personification.

pathos: along with *ethos* and *logos*, one of the three categories of appeal that are set out in classical *rhetoric*. The word "pathos" is sometimes thought to hold pejorative *connotations*—to describe an appeal to the emotions that is too contrived, too blatant, or too superficial. Appeals to the emotions may surely be all of those things. But they need not be any of them—and certainly the term "pathos," properly used, carries much the same meaning today as it did for the ancients, referring to any appeal to the emotions. The emotional quality of a *discourse*, and the ability of a discourse to appeal to our emotions—these are central to the concept of pathos.

pattern poetry: an early predecessor of modern *concrete poetry* in which the shape of the poem on the page is intended to suggest or imitate an aspect of the poem's subject. George Herbert's 1633 poem "Easter Wings" is perhaps the best-known example of pattern poetry.

penny dreadful: Victorian publication in serial form intended for popular consumption, with each weekly number published in pamphlet form, priced at one penny. Often aimed at an adolescent audience, penny dreadfuls were often reprints or simplified versions of already-popular novels. Typically they were sensational in subject matter; among the more popular long-running penny dreadfuls were *Varney the Vampire* and *The String of Pearls*, which told the story of Sweeney Todd, the "demon barber of Fleet Street." Not all penny dreadfuls were works of fiction; many recounted true or allegedly true stories of crime and horror.

pentameter: a line of verse containing five metrical *feet*.

perfect rhyme: see *rhyme*.

performance poetry: poetry composed primarily for oral performance, often very theatrical in nature. See also *dub poetry* and *rap*.

performative utterance: speech that also constitutes the performance of an action (e.g., "I arrest you"; "I do" during a marriage ceremony).

periodic sentence: sentence in which the main idea appears just before the period at the end, with various supporting or qualifying ideas appearing in subordinate clauses and phrases prior to that. A staple of the grand style of oratory, the periodic sentence may also be used playfully, as in this example: "Whether in the chill of spring or the heat of summer, whether in youth or age, whether all of us together or each on their own, whether at Wrigley Field or far from any ballpark, whether sober or not-so-much-so, we shall always follow our beloved Chicago Cubs." The opposite of a periodic sentence is a "loose" sentence, in which the subject and verb appear first.

peripeteia: in literature, a swift reversal of a character's position or circumstances, especially one leading to the ruin of the protagonist in a tragedy. Aristotle, who discussed the concept in his *Poetics*, argued that the moment of peripeteia ideally should be unforeseen by both the character and the audience, but should nonetheless follow logically from preceding events.

peroration: in classical *rhetoric*, the conclusion to a speech—typically the part in which the orator would do most to stir the emotions of his audience.

persona: the assumed identity or "speaking voice" that a writer projects in a *discourse*. The term "persona" literally means "mask."

personification: a *figure of speech* (a *trope*), also known as "prosopopoeia," in which a writer refers to inanimate objects, ideas, or animals as if they were human, or creates a human figure to represent an abstract entity such as Philosophy or Peace.

Petrarch, Francesco: see *sonnet (Italian / Petrarchan)*.

Petrarchan sonnet: see *humanism / Renaissance humanism*, *octave*, *sestet*, *sonnet (Italian / Petrarchan)*.

philistine: pejorative term used to denote a person ignorant of artistic or intellectual pursuits, and holding views antithetical to those pursuits.

phoneme: a linguistic term denoting the smallest unit of sound that it is possible to distinguish. The one-syllable words *fun* and *phone* each have three phonemes, though one has three letters and one has five.

picaresque narrative: adventure fiction made up of a series of episodes and often satirical in content. The form developed in sixteenth-century Spain and originates from the Spanish word *pícaro* (meaning "rogue" or "scoundrel"), referring to the appealingly roguish protagonists such works typically employ. Examples in English include Daniel Defoe's *Moll Flanders* (1722) and, arguably, Henry Fielding's *Joseph Andrews* (1742) and *Tom Jones* (1749). Considered a precursor to or early form of the novel, picaresque fiction was superseded by the novel in the late eighteenth century, but the adjective "picaresque" is sometimes applied to later novels with picaresque elements, such as Mark Twain's *Adventures of Huckleberry Finn* (1884).

Pico della Mirandola, Giovanni: see *humanism / Renaissance humanism*.

Pindar: see *ode, strophe*.

Pindaric: see *ode*.

p

plagiarism: unacknowledged "borrowing" in one's own writing of the words and ideas of another (or others). "Borrowing" is here a *euphemistic* term; "theft" is more accurate, and truer to the term's Latin origin in a word meaning "to kidnap."

Plath, Sylvia: see *confessional poetry*.

Plato: see *mimesis, Neo-Platonism*.

plot: the organization of story materials within a literary work. The order in which story material is presented; the inclusion of elements that allow or encourage the reader or audience to form expectations as to what is likely to happen; the decision to present some story material through *exposition* rather than present it directly to the reader as part of the narrative—all these are matters of plotting.

In Aristotle's famous formulation in the *Poetics*, a plot must have a beginning, a middle, and an end in order to be "whole":

> a beginning is that which does not itself follow anything by causal necessity, but after which something naturally is or comes to be. An end, on the contrary, is that which itself naturally follows some other thing, either by necessity, or as a rule, but has nothing following it. A middle is that which follows something as some other thing follows it. A well constructed plot, therefore, must neither begin nor end at haphazard, but conform to these principles.

"Nothing following it" cannot of course be taken literally; *they lived happily ever after* is not nothing. Rather it suggests that there is no mesh of causes, or of conflicts, or of unresolved intentions extending into a future beyond the end of the plot.

Plotting as Aristotle described it has been the dominant mode in English literature since the late sixteenth century—though *episodic plotting* has also been common.

Poe, Edgar Allan: see *grotesque*.

poetic diction: elevated language, considered in some eras to be particularly appropriate to poetry. To say "verdant glebe" rather than "green field," for example, is to use poetic diction.

poetic justice: when, at the conclusion of a literary work, good characters are rewarded (and bad ones not), it is said that poetic justice has been done. The phrase dates from the late seventeenth century, but the notion that it would be inappropriate not to see virtue rewarded in a literary work has its roots in classical Greece.

poetics: analysis of and/or theorizing as to the principles of creative writing and literary form; the founding work of the genre is Aristotle's fourth-century BCE treatise *Poetics*. Note that "poetics" concerns all forms of literature, not just poetry; the root is the Greek verb meaning "to make, to invent."

point of view: see *narrative perspective.*

polyphonic: literally, "many voiced." Polyphonic music has more than one line of melody. When a literary work is said to be polyphonic, it typically gives expression to multiple points of view and has numerous threads of story.

polysyndeton: the inclusion for rhetorical or literary purposes of extra conjunctions that are not necessary to a sentence's grammatical construction. In the following example from Adrienne Rich's "Living in Sin" (1955), the repetitions of "and" are an example of polysyndeton: "she, jeered by the minor demons, / pulled back the sheets and made the bed and found / a towel to dust the table-top, / and let the coffee-pot boil over on the stove."

Pontormo, Jacopo: see *mannerism.*

Pope, Alexander: see *alexandrine, anticlimax, antithesis, endstopped, georgic, mock-heroic, zeugma.*

Popper, Karl: see *historicism / new historicism.*

portmanteau word: Just as portmanteau luggage is made up of two compartments, a portmanteau word is made up through a combination of two existing words. *Guesstimate* is now a well-established portmanteau word—as is *brunch*. An alternative term is "blend."

postcolonial theory / postcolonial studies: an interdisciplinary and diverse body of thought addressing the effects of Western colonialism and imperialism—effects that postcolonial thinkers argue are ongoing long after official decolonization. "Postcolonialism" is sometimes taken to mean "after the end of colonialism"—that is, after decolonization—but many postcolonial thinkers also study the history of colonization. Some theorists in this area question whether the term "postcolonial" should be used at all, arguing that it falsely suggests that the West no longer culturally, politically, and economically dominates other areas of the world.

Although postcolonial studies also engages with economic, material, and political inequality between the West and its former colonies, one of its primary objects is to better understand the cultural dimension of colonialism and its continued effects: how a colonizing culture's language, ways of being, and ways of knowing are imposed on a colonized culture, and how decolonized nations can resist and recover from that cultural damage. Postcolonial theorists also consider how the blending of cultures and the movement of people across the globe change the way we think about cultural identity—how cultures interact with each other, and how groups and individuals negotiate those interactions.

Postcolonial studies incorporates multiple disciplines; postcolonial historians, for example, attempt to correct the historical record's Western bias by writing histories with a focus on the perspectives and experiences of colonized peoples. Postcolonial literary criticism is the study of how colonization, colonizers, and colonized people are represented in literature—both in works that take up explicitly anti-colonial themes, and in works that reinforce colonial attitudes.

postmodernism: in literature and the visual arts, a movement influential in the late twentieth and early twenty-first centuries. In some ways postmodernism represents a reaction to *modernism*, in others an extension of it. With roots in the work of French philosophers such as Jacques Derrida (1930-2004) and Michel Foucault (1926-84), it is deeply colored by theory; indeed, it may be said to have begun at the "meta" level of theorizing rather than at the level of practice. It is notoriously resistant to definition— indeed, resistance to fixed definitions is itself a characteristic of postmodernism. Like modernism, postmodernism embraces difficulty and distrusts the simple and straightforward. More broadly, postmodernism is characterized by a rejection of absolute truth or value, of closed systems, of grand unified narratives.

Postmodernist fiction is characterized by a frequently ironic or playful tone in dealing with reality and illusion; by a willingness to combine different styles or forms in a single work (just as in architecture the postmodernist spirit embodies a willingness to borrow from seemingly disparate styles in designing a single structure); and by a highly attuned awareness of the problematized state of the writer, artist, or theorist as observer.

poststructuralism: see *structuralism / poststructuralism*.

Pound, Ezra: see *avant-garde, free verse, futurism, Imagism, language poetry, modernism, Vorticism*.

practical criticism: In the 1920s, I.A. Richards (1893-1979) carried out a series of experiments with his Cambridge students, asking them a variety of critical and interpretive questions about literary works, without giving them any information as to when or where or by whom the works had been written. They were thus encouraged to concentrate on the work itself in a way that, Richards suggested, could be more fruitful—even more practical—than it was to give readers a good deal of historical and biographical information beforehand, as had been common practice. Richards called the 1929 book in which he reported on these experiments *Practical Criticism*, and the concept became highly influential during the era of *New Criticism* and *close reading*.

Pre-Raphaelites: originally, a group of Victorian artists and writers, formed in 1848. Their goal was to revive what they considered the simpler, fresher, and more natural art that had existed before the time of the Italian painter Raphael (1483-1520). The poet Dante Gabriel Rossetti (1828-82) was one of the founders of the group.

prescriptive: intended largely or entirely to dictate how things should be done, how people should behave, etc. If a dictionary is prescriptive it instructs readers as to how they should use language; if it is descriptive it aims merely to describe how language is in fact used.

print culture / history of the book: The past generation has seen greatly increased interest in the history of the book—and, more broadly, in what has come to be called "print culture." "Print culture" is an umbrella term under which a very broad range of phenomena may be studied. The differences between cultures of orality (as Walter Ong termed them) and print cultures as a whole is one obvious point of focus. The development of the printing press in the fifteenth century—and the history of book production thereafter—is another. The ways in which electronic texts may be both likened to and contrasted with paper texts is a central concern among many studying print culture in the twenty-first century.

p

Other topics that are important parts of the study of print culture include the ways in which print culture has participated in the spread of ideas in general—and, more particularly, in the development of particular political and economic systems; the growth of the mass media in the nineteenth and twentieth centuries (the study of print culture of course embraces the study of newspapers, magazines, and pamphlets as well as that of books); the history of copyright, and the effect of copyright laws on cultural production; the role printed works have played in the construction of ideology; and the interaction in drama and film between printed texts and the implied text of a performance.

In addition to Ong (1912-2003), important founding figures in the study of print culture include Raymond Williams, whose *The Long Revolution* (1961) argued that the growth of literacy had a greater effect on human society than did the industrial revolution; Marshall McLuhan, whose *The Gutenberg Galaxy: The Making of Typographic Man* (1962) speculated that the printing press was the primary agent for many different changes, including the rise of nationalism, the rise of scientific rationalism, and a "global village" mentality; and Elizabeth Eisenstein, whose *The Printing Press as an Agent of Change* (1979) adopted a more conventional historian's approach in tackling many of the same subjects.

The study of print culture brings together academics studying literary and economic history with those engaged in literary theory. In many cases history and theory may coexist within the same work. An influential 1993 article by Margreta de Grazia and Peter Stallybrass which appeared in *Shakespeare Quarterly* may serve as an example. Until the late twentieth century the typical practice in editing a Shakespearian text of which more than one version existed was to produce a hybrid text, with the editors choosing among different possible readings the ones that seemed to them to "make the most sense." In a case such as *King Lear*, where very substantially different printed texts exist in the Folio and Quarto editions, that process necessarily involves a high degree of editorial intervention. In "The Materiality of the Shakespeare Text," de Grazia and Stallybrass argue against such practices—not because they may get us no closer to what we may imagine to have been Shakespeare's intention, but because in their very "materiality," texts such as the different early versions of *King Lear* "insist upon being looked *at*, not seen *through*"—that in their specifics, such texts "cannot comply with modern notions of correctness and intelligibility."

problem play: a play that examines ethical and societal issues, typically in a naturalistic, contemporary setting. Problem plays developed in the late nineteenth century and are still written in the twenty-first; well-known authors of problem plays include Henrik Ibsen (1828-1906), Bernard Shaw (1856-1950), and Arthur Miller (1915-2005).

In the context of scholarly criticism, the term "problem play" can also refer to plays that are difficult to categorize. Shakespeare's plays *Measure for Measure*, *All's Well That Ends Well*, and *Troilus and Cressida* are often described as "problem plays," in part because they have characteristics of both comedy and tragedy.

prolepsis: originally a rhetorical term, used to refer to the anticipation of possible objections by someone advancing an argument, "prolepsis" is used in discussions of fiction to refer to elements in a narrative that anticipate the future of the story. The *flashforward* technique of storytelling is often described as a form of prolepsis; the inclusion in a narrative of material that *foreshadows* future developments is also sometimes treated as a form of prolepsis.

prompt book: the prompter's copy of a script of a play, containing cues for light and sound; the entrances, exits, and actions of the performers; and any other information required to run the performance.

propaganda: though this term is often used pejoratively to imply that a work has little or no literary value, it need not carry any negative connotations; the core meaning of "propaganda" is simply writing that, in addressing a particular political or ethical issue, aims to persuade the reader (or audience) to support a particular position. See also *agitprop*.

Propp, Vladimir: see *narratology / narrative theory*.

proscenium: a Latin architectural term derived from the Greek *proskenion*, the frontmost section of the theater building (*skēnē*) as it developed in the post-Classical, *Hellenistic* period. Stages on which a pictorial illusion is created with the help of a border or frame are called "proscenium arch" or "picture-frame" theaters; they reached their heyday during the nineteenth century, the age of *realism*.

prose poem: a poetic discourse that uses prose formats (e.g., it may use margins and paragraphs rather than line breaks or stanzas) yet is written with the kind of attention to language, rhythm, and cadence that characterizes verse.

prosody: the study and analysis of meter, rhythm, rhyme, stanzaic pattern, and other devices of versification.

prosopopoeia: see *personification*.

protagonist: the central character in a literary work.

prothalamion: a wedding song; a term coined by the poet Edmund Spenser (1552-99), adapted from *epithalamion*.

psychoanalytic criticism: a term that describes a variety of critical approaches based on the work of Sigmund Freud (1856-1939), or on that of later thinkers who have extended or critiqued Freud's work. As a psychological treatment method, psychoanalysis focuses on repressed ideas and emotions in the patient's unconscious mind, with particular attention to early childhood, traumatic experiences, and sexual development and desire. Psychoanalytic criticism adapts this approach to the study of literature and other cultural products. Often, this has meant psychoanalyzing fictional characters to reveal their unconscious *motivations*, or psychoanalyzing authors to understand their works as manifestations of neuroses or unconscious desires— approaches that are still used, but are less common in the twenty- first century than they were for much of the twentieth.

Psychoanalytic criticism since the 1950s has been profoundly influenced by the work of Jacques Lacan (1901-81), who com- bined *Freudian* psychology with *structuralism*. For Lacan, each individual's sense of being a coherent, conscious "self" is a delu- sion, hiding the fact that the psyche is highly fragmented and is dominated by an unconscious that cannot be accessed directly or controlled. Lacan was deeply interested in the relationship between language, the unconscious, and the illusion of self- hood—and in the ways that the structure of the mind parallels the structure of language. Because of its linguistic focus, his work is well suited to applications in literary criticism; he has been particularly influential among *poststructuralist* thinkers such as Jacques Derrida (1930-2004), Hélène Cixous (b. 1937), and Julia Kristeva (b. 1941).

Psychoanalytic criticism also includes a wide range of other approaches. Freud's student Carl Jung's (1875-1961) concept of the "collective unconscious," for example, informs some critics' study of *archetypes*—*motifs*, characters, and other elements that recur across cultures in literature and mythology. (See also *mytho- poeic theory and criticism*.)

pun: a play on words, in which a word with two or more distinct meanings, or two words with similar sounds, may create humor- ous ambiguities. Also known as "paranomasia."

pyrrhic foot: a metrical *foot* containing two weak stresses: x x.

quantitative meter: a metrical system used by Greek and Roman poets, in which a line of verse was measured by the *quantity*, or length of sound, of each syllable. A *foot* was measured in terms of syllables classed as long or short.

quantity: duration of syllables in poetry. The line "There is a Garden in her face" (the first line from the 1617 poem of the same name by Thomas Campion) is characterized by the short quantities of the syllables. The last line of Thomas Hardy's 1917 poem "During Wind and Rain" has the same number of syllables as the line by Campion, but the quantities of the syllables are much longer—in other words, the line takes much longer to say: "Down their carved names the rain drop ploughs."

quarto: a book made by printing large sheets and folding them twice to produce eight pages per sheet; it is half the size of a *folio* book, which is made by folding large sheets once to produce four pages per sheet. The terms "quarto" and "folio" are often used in the context of Shakespeare to indicate different editions of his work; many of Shakespeare's individual plays were published in quarto during his lifetime, while his collected plays were published in folio after his death.

quatrain: a four-line stanza, usually rhymed.

queer theory: a diverse body of thought that emerged in the early 1990s, combining influences from many sources including *feminist theory*, *postcolonial theory*, gay studies, and the work of *poststructuralist* theorists such as Michel Foucault (1926-84). Many queer theorists seek to undermine the idea that sex and gender categories (i.e., male, female, heterosexual) are natural or stable, arguing instead that these categories are cre-

p

ated and imposed upon people by social structures; the set of forces that imposes these categories—and their attendant rules of heterosexual, monogamous marriage—is sometimes called "heteronormativity."

Queer theory is most commonly associated with the societal positions of gay, lesbian, bisexual, transgendered, and other people who display non-normative gender or sexuality, but it is also extended to issues such as race, class, and ability/disability, especially in terms of their intersection with issues of sexuality and gender. In fact, queer theory is sometimes employed to destabilize identity categories in general, revealing that no individuals ever fully embody the identities that are imposed on them by cultural norms. Queer theory can also refer to a methodology called "queering," which can be applied to any text; to "queer" a text means to point out and analyze instabilities in its norms and categories relating to sex and gender identity.

Queer theory is sometimes aligned with the activities of gay, lesbian, and other activist groups—especially those groups that take a more confrontational approach to activism and want to avoid assimilation with mainstream society. However, many activists and academics question queer theory's political effectiveness, arguing that it undermines identity positions, which are important for building activist and intellectual communities with shared goals and a coherent message. Many queer theorists, on the other hand, are interested in the ways in which people and groups might be able to have political agency without subordinating themselves to gender, sexual, and other norms.

Important thinkers associated with queer theory include Eve Kosofsky Sedgwick (1950-2009), Judith Butler (b. 1956), Michael Warner (b. 1958), and Teresa de Lauretis (b. 1938).

Quiller-Couch, Sir Arthur: see *New Criticism*.

quintet: a five-line stanza. Sometimes given as "quintain."

Ransom, John Crowe: see *New Criticism*.

rap: originally coined to describe informal conversation, "rap" now usually describes a style of *performance poetry* in which a poet will chant rhymed verse, sometimes improvised and usually with musical accompaniment that has a heavy beat.

Raphael (Raffaello Sanzio da Urbino): see *Pre-Raphaelites*.

reader response criticism / reader response theory: a branch of theory and criticism that studies how readers interpret and respond to texts. Reader response theory and criticism developed in the 1960s and 1970s, primarily in North America and Germany. Its advocates argue that there is no such thing as an objective text that can be objectively interpreted—instead, every text offers an effectively unlimited range of possible meanings, and actual meaning is produced only through interpretation when a reader interacts with a text. Some reader response critics collect and study the responses of real individuals to texts, focusing on the ways in which subjective experience leads to differences in individuals' interpretations. Other critics theorize the existence of abstract readers and base their criticism on the theoretical reader's response. Still others—notably Stanley Fish (b. 1938)—consider how social groups function as "interpretive communities," which establish an agreed-upon meaning for a given text through shared interpretation; according to this approach, multiple interpretive communities exist at any one time, and as a society's interpretive communities evolve and are replaced, texts will take on different meanings.

realism: as a literary term, the presentation through literature of material closely resembling real life. As notions both of what constitutes "real life" and of how it may be most faithfully represented in literature have varied widely, "realism" has taken a variety of meanings. The term "naturalistic" has sometimes been used a synonym for "realistic"; *naturalism* originated in the nineteenth century as a term denoting a form of realism focusing in particular on grim, unpleasant, or ugly aspects of the real.

Reaney, James: see *mythopoeic theory and criticism*.

recto: the front side of a page—or, in a bound book, the right-side pages; the opposite is *verso*, which refers to the back sides of loose pages or the left-side pages in a book.

referent: the real-world thing that is referred to by a word or phrase. Some theorists argue that a referent must be a concrete object (such as a physical pencil referred to by the word "pencil"), while others also consider abstract concepts (such as the concept of freedom) to be referents. Theorists distinguish a word's referential meaning—the meaning the word has through its relation to a thing outside of language—from its sense, the meaning it has through its relationship to other words.

refrain: one or more words or lines repeated at regular points throughout a poem, often at the end of each stanza or group of stanzas. Sometimes a whole stanza may be repeated to create a refrain, like the chorus in a song.

Regan, Tom: see *animal studies*.

reggae: a style of heavily rhythmic music from the West Indies with lyrics that are colloquial in language and often anti-establishment in content and flavor. First popularized in the 1960s and 1970s, reggae has had a lasting influence on *performance poetry*, *rap*, and *dub*.

Rembrandt van Rijn: see *baroque*.

r

r

Renaissance: literally, "rebirth"; roughly speaking, the term refers to a flourishing of intellectual and artistic development that occurred in Europe in the fifteenth and sixteenth centuries, during which European culture transitioned from the medieval period to the modern era. Significant developments associated with the Renaissance include increased interest in and widespread access to classical works; increased individualism and secularism; scientific discoveries, especially in astronomy; and the exploration of what became North and South America. The term "Renaissance" is also used more specifically to refer to the Italian Renaissance of the early fourteenth to early sixteenth centuries; the Renaissance in England is generally considered to have occurred somewhat later, in the late sixteenth and early seventeenth centuries, although some scholars question whether or not England experienced anything that can be properly termed a "Renaissance." See also *humanism*.

"Renaissance" can also refer more generally to a time of cultural flourishing. For example, the term *"Harlem Renaissance"* refers to a movement of African-American writers, artists, and musicians that occurred in the 1920s and 1930s in Harlem and elsewhere in the United States, while the *"Irish Literary Renaissance"* of the late nineteenth and early twentieth centuries centered on the celebration and revival of ancient Irish culture.

Restoration comedy: a type of comic play that flourished in the late seventeenth century in London (following the restoration of the monarchy and the re-opening of the theaters after the Puritan interregnum under Oliver Cromwell), in which the comedy is typically based on the sexual and marital intrigues of "high society." Leading Restoration comic playwrights include Aphra Behn (1640-89), William Wycherley (1641-1715), and William Congreve (1670-1729).

rhetoric: in classical Greece and Rome, the art of persuasion and public speaking. From the Middle Ages onwards, the study of rhetoric gave greater attention to style, particularly *figures of speech*. Today in *poetics*, the term "rhetoric" may encompass not only figures of speech, but also the persuasive effects of forms, sounds, and word choices.

rhyme: the repetition of identical or similar sounds, usually in pairs and generally at the ends of metrical lines. In English, a full (or perfect) rhyme must involve the final stressed syllable of a line—as in this example:

> The grass was dark, the moon was round,
> And he lay dead upon the ground.

It must also involve vowel as well as consonant sounds. In the following example the ending consonant sounds (-*nd*) match, but the ending vowel sounds are different:

> The grass was dark, the moon was round,
> And he had finally met his end.

In most lines of English poetry the final syllable in a line is also the final stressed syllable of the line—but in many lines that is not the case. In the following example both vowel and consonant sounds match in the final syllables of the lines, but the lines nevertheless do not rhyme; the final stressed syllables (*go-* and *end-*) have quite different sounds:

> The grass was dark, the light was going,
> And on the ground his life was ending.

In summary, then: for there to be a full rhyme in English, the vowel sounds as well as the ending consonant sounds of the final syllable must match, and the same must be true of the final stressed syllable, if that is different.

Following is a list of some other terms used in connection with rhyme.

r

end-rhyme: a rhyming word or syllable at the end of a line.

eye rhyme: rhyming that pairs words whose spellings are alike but whose pronunciations are different: for example, "though" / "slough."

feminine rhyme: a two-syllable (also known as "double") rhyme. The first syllable is stressed and the second unstressed: for example, "hasty" / "tasty." See also *triple rhyme* below.

interlocking rhyme: the repetition of rhymes from one stanza to the next, creating links that add to the poem's continuity and coherence. Examples may be found in Shelley's use of *terza rima* in "Ode to the West Wind" (1819) and in Dylan Thomas's *villanelle* "Do Not Go Gentle into That Good Night" (1951).

internal rhyme: the placement of rhyming words within lines so that at least two words in a line rhyme with each other.

masculine rhyme: a correspondence of sound between the final stressed syllables at the end of two or more lines, as in "grieve" / "leave," "ar-rive" / "sur-vive."

partial rhyme: There can be several forms of partial rhyme. There are also several terms widely used to refer to any form of partial rhyme—among them "near rhyme," "imperfect rhyme," "half-rhyme," and "slant rhyme." Here are some of the forms of partial rhyme:

- unstressed syllables may match but not stressed ones (e.g., "water" / "flower"); this is also known as "weak" or "unstressed rhyme."

- a stressed syllable may be "rhymed" with an unstressed one (e.g., "sing" / "casing").

- one of the rhymed words may have an "extra" syllable at the end (e.g., "clink" / "drinking").

- the match in sound may be imperfect (e.g., "grin" / "plain"); this is sometimes referred to as "forced rhyme," or "oblique rhyme."

- the consonant sounds of stressed syllables match, but the vowel sounds do not (e.g., "spoiled" / "spilled," "taint" / "stint"). This form of partial rhyme is sometimes referred to as "slant rhyme"—though slant rhyme is also sometimes used as a term to denote any form of partial rhyme.

triple rhyme: a three-syllable rhyme in which the first syllable of each rhyme-word is stressed and the other two unstressed (e.g., "lottery" / "coterie").

true rhyme: a rhyme in which everything but the initial consonant matches perfectly in sound and spelling.

rhyme royal: a stanza of seven *iambic pentameters*, with a rhyme scheme of *ababbcc*. This is also known as the "Chaucerian stanza," as Chaucer was the first English poet to use this form. See also *septet*.

rhyme scheme: the pattern of *rhyme* (usually *end-rhyme*) in a stanza, whole poem, or song. Rhyme schemes are commonly recorded as a series of letters, one for each line, in which lines that rhyme with each other receive the same letter. For example, a rhyming couplet has the rhyme scheme *aa*, while a Shakespearean sonnet has the rhyme scheme *abab cdcd efef gg*.

rhythm: In speech, the arrangement of stressed and unstressed syllables creates units of sound. In song or verse, these units usually form a regular rhythmic pattern, a kind of beat, described in *prosody* as *meter*.

Ricardian literature: the literature of late-fourteenth-century England. In other contexts, "Ricardian" can refer to the reign of Richard I, II, or III, but in literary studies it is most commonly used to denote the period of Richard II's reign (1377-99).

Rice, Anne: see *Gothic*.

Rich, Adrienne: see *polysyndeton*.

Richard II: see *Ricardian literature*.

Richards, I.A.: see *New Criticism, practical criticism*.

Richardson, Dorothy: see *stream of consciousness*.

Richardson, Samuel: see *epistolary novel*.

Ricœur, Paul: see *narratology / narrative theory*.

Rilke, Rainer Maria: see *Neo-Platonism*.

Rimbaud, Arthur: see *symbolist movement*.

rising action: see *Freytag's pyramid*.

rising rhythm: a pattern of rhythm in which syllables flow from unstressed to stressed; *iambic* and *anapestic* meters tend to display this pattern. In English verse, rising rhythm is much more usual than its opposite, *falling rhythm*, in which syllables flow from stressed to unstressed.

rococo: see *baroque*.

roman à clef: a novel in which one key to the reader's understanding is the knowledge that one or more of the characters are thinly veiled representations of real people. (The French *roman à clef* literally means "novel with a key.") In Robert Penn Warren's acclaimed novel *All the King's Men* (1946), for example, the populist governor Willie Stark is transparently modeled on Louisiana governor Huey Long.

romance: Medieval romance, a genre that flourished from the twelfth to fifteenth centuries, often incorporates adventure, courtly love, and suspension of the ordinary laws of nature (e.g., magic or fantastic beings); earlier romances of this sort were written in verse, while later ones were more frequently written in prose. *Sir Gawain and the Green Knight* and *Le Morte d'Arthur* are particularly well-known examples of the genre.

The term "romance" is also sometimes applied to later works that share some of the adventurous and/or supernatural elements of medieval romance, including the *Gothic* novel, the *sentimental* novel, *fantasy*, and *science fiction*. In contemporary popular usage, "romance novel" usually refers to a novel centered on a love relationship.

Roman literature: see *acts [of a play]*, *carpe diem*, *deus ex machina*, *Horatian ode*, *humanism / Renaissance humanism*, *Latinate*, *ode*, *palimpsest*, *pastoral*, *quantitative meter*, *rhetoric*, *theater-in-the-round*.

Romanticism: a major social and cultural movement, originating in Europe, that shaped much of Western artistic thought in the late eighteenth and nineteenth centuries. Opposing the ideal of controlled, rational order associated with the Enlightenment, Romanticism emphasizes the importance of spontaneous self-expression, emotion, and personal experience in producing art. In Romanticism, the "natural" is privileged over the conventional or the artificial.

rondeau: a fifteen-line poem, generally *octosyllabic*, with only two rhymes throughout its three stanzas, and an unrhymed refrain at the end of the ninth and fifteenth lines, repeating part of the opening line. Although the form was most popular in medieval court music, it continues to be employed by poets; a well-known example is John McCrae's "In Flanders Fields" (1915).

Rossetti, Dante Gabriel: see *ballade, Pre-Raphaelites*.

Rosso Fiorentino: see *mannerism*.

Rothko, Mark: see *expressionism / impressionism*.

Rouault, Georges: see *expressionism / impressionism*.

round character: a complex and psychologically realistic character, often one who changes as a fiction progresses. The opposite of a round character is a *flat character*.

Rowling, J.K.: see *fantasy*.

rune: a letter of the Old Germanic alphabet, used by people of Northern Europe, beginning in the second century CE, for inscriptions and the casting of spells. The term is sometimes used more generally to refer to magic symbols.

Rushdie, Salman: see *magic realism*.

Russian formalism: an early-twentieth-century movement among Russian critics and theorists that paid close attention to the features of literary language—especially that of poetry. Certain Russian formalists, Victor Shklovsky (1893-1984) chief among them, paid close attention to prose fiction as well, focusing especially on the means whereby literature may *defamiliarize* the reader's world.

Said, Edward: see *essay, Orientalism.*

Sapphic: a stanza form named after the ancient Greek poet Sappho (seventh-sixth century BCE). In ancient Greek, the *meter* of each line is determined by its pattern of "long" and "short" syllables, but present-day Sapphics are written in a pattern of stressed and unstressed syllables. Each Sapphic stanza consists of three eleven-syllable lines, usually patterned / x / x / x x / x / x (although the fourth and last syllables can sometimes be stressed), and one five-syllable line patterned either / x x / x or / x x / /.

Sappho: see *Sapphic.*

sarcasm: a particularly straightforward or crude form of *irony* (usually spoken), in which the meaning is conveyed largely by the tone of voice adopted; something said sarcastically is meant clearly to imply its opposite.

satire: literary work designed to make fun of or seriously criticize its subject. According to many literary theories of the *Renaissance* and *neoclassical* periods, the ridicule through satire of a certain sort of behavior may function for the reader or audience as a corrective of such behavior.

Saussure, Ferdinand de: see *semiotics, structuralism / poststructuralism.*

scansion: the formal analysis of patterns of rhythm and rhyme in poetry. Each line of verse will have a certain number of fairly regular "beats" consisting of alternating stressed and unstressed syllables. To "scan" a poem is to count the beats in each line, to mark stressed and unstressed syllables and indicate their combination into *feet*, to note pauses, and to identify rhyme schemes with letters of the alphabet (e.g., *abab*).

scheme: see *figures of speech*.

Schiele, Egon: see *expressionism / impressionism*.

science fiction: fiction featuring imaginary science and technology and/or imaginatively exploring the possible implications of scientific knowledge (e.g., extraterrestrial civilizations, environmental destruction, genetic mutations, etc.), usually within the context of a future, distant, or alternative world. A distinction is sometimes made between "hard" science fiction, in which elements of real or fictional science are thoroughly explained, and "soft" science fiction, in which the science itself is given less prominence than the exploration of a society or of individual characters. The history of science fiction extends at least as far back as Mary Shelley's *Frankenstein* (1818) and the late-nineteenth-century works of H.G. Wells and Jules Verne, but the term "science fiction" itself entered popular usage in the 1920s.

It is often imagined that works of science fiction are, almost by definition, set in some future world, but there is in fact no necessary connection between the two; science fiction may in some instances involve a recreation of an imagined past, and it may also be set in imaginary worlds that are outside of time as we know it.

The term "science fiction" is sometimes used interchangeably with the term *speculative fiction*, but not all works of science fiction are speculative in nature, and not all works of speculative fiction involve scientific content.

Sedgwick, Eve Kosofsky: see *affect, feminism / feminist criticism and theory / gender-based criticism and theory*.

semantics: in logic or linguistics, the study of meaning in relation to language. Among the questions addressed by semantics are whether and how words correspond to things in the real world; how language is interpreted; and how the context in which words are used contributes to their meaning. (In colloquial usage, the phrase "that's just semantics" is often used to suggest that an argument or a distinction that has been put forward turns on nothing more than trivial issues of word choice, rather than anything related to underlying meaning.)

semiotics: the study of language as a system of "signs." A major figure in the development of semiotics is Ferdinand de Saussure (1857-1913), who defined a "sign" as a pairing of "signifier" (i.e., the sound and written appearance of a word) and "signified" (i.e., the concept to which the word refers). According to Saussure, the relationship between any given signifier and its signified is arbitrary—there is, for example, no resemblance between the sound or appearance of the word "table" and the physical object itself. Signs do not derive their meaning from their relationship to things in the real world, but instead have meaning only as part of a relational system—that is, through their differences from other signs.

Another important concept in Saussure's work is the distinction between "langue"—the grammatical and other conventions of a language, comprising a system that determines all the possible things that can be said or written in that language—and "parole," actual instances of speech and writing.

A "signifier" can be a word, but can also be a gesture, image, or any other unit that carries meaning, so a semiotic approach can be used to study any cultural practice. For example, the influential critic Roland Barthes (1915-80) applied semiotics to the study of such diverse "texts" as Balzac's novella *Sarrasine* (1830), French fries, and professional wrestling. See *structuralism*.

sensation literature: a subgenre of the novel that was enormously popular during the 1860s and incorporated shocking and suspenseful elements—such as crime (especially murder and sexual crime), family secrets, and insanity—within the setting of respectable Victorian society. Well-known examples include Wilkie Collins's *The Woman in White* (1860) and Mary Elizabeth Braddon's *Lady Audley's Secret* (1862).

sensibility: see *sentiment.*

sentiment: In present-day colloquial usage, "sentiment" means "emotion," often with the negative *connotation* of "excessive emotion." In the later eighteenth century, however—and in the study of eighteenth-century literature and philosophy— "sentiment" refers to moral feeling understood as the basis of virtuous behavior. The philosophical concept of sentiment (also called "sensibility") reflected a belief in the innate goodness of human beings, thought to be reflected in an individual's emotional responses—although some thinkers saw sentiment as requiring the exercise of reason in conjunction with appropriate feeling.

The concept of sentiment was explored in such literary subgenres as the "sentimental novel" and, in drama, the "sentimental comedy"; both sentimental novels and sentimental comedies feature emotionally intense scenes and highly virtuous characters whose emotional expressiveness is presented as evidence of their goodness. By the beginning of the nineteenth century, sentiment had already taken on some of its present-day negative connotation, and many works of this period—perhaps most famously, Jane Austen's *Sense and Sensibility* (1811)—react against sentimental literature.

septet: a stanza containing seven lines.

sestet: a six-line stanza that forms the second grouping of lines in a Petrarchan *sonnet*, following the *octave*. See *sonnet (Italian / Petrarchan)* and *sestina*.

sestina: an elaborate unrhymed poem with six six-line stanzas (*sestets*) and a three-line *envoy*.

setting: the time, place, and cultural environment in which a story takes place.

Sewell, Anna: see *animal studies*.

Sexton, Anne: see *confessional poetry*.

Shakespeare, William: see *apocryphal, bowdlerize, elision, folio, historicism / new historicism, interior monologue, metaphor, negative capability, New Criticism, problem play, quarto, rhyme scheme, sonnet (Shakespearean), soliloquy, stichomythia, substitution*.

Shakespearean sonnet: see *sonnet (Shakespearean)*.

Shavian: part of or similar to the work or thought of Bernard Shaw (1856-1950), an Irish dramatist, novelist, and critic best known for his often satirical and controversial plays addressing social issues. Shavian can also refer more specifically to the characteristic wit of Shaw's dialogue and *epigrams*.

Shaw, Bernard: see *problem play, Shavian*.

Shelley, Mary: see *feminism / feminist criticism and theory / gender-based criticism and theory, frame narrative, science fiction*.

Shelley, Percy Bysshe: see *elegy, Neo-Platonism, interlocking rhyme, terza rima*.

Sheridan, Richard Brinsley: see *malapropism*.

Shklovsky, Victor: see *Russian Formalism*.

Sholokhov, Mikhail: see *Marxist theory and criticism*.

short story: see *novel*.

Sidney, Sir Philip: see *apology, novel*.

simile: a *figure of speech* (a *trope*) that makes an explicit comparison between a particular object and another object or idea that is similar in some (often unexpected) way. A simile always uses "like" or "as" to signal the connection. Compare with *metaphor*.

Sinclair, May: see *stream of consciousness*.

Singer, Peter: see *animal studies*.

Slam Poetry: "Spoken word" or "*performance*" poetry presented in competitions ("slams") and judged by the audience. The practice began in Chicago bars and cafes in the mid-1980s.

slant rhyme: see *rhyme*.

soft landing: see *feminine ending*.

soliloquy: in drama (or, less often, poetry), a speech in which a character, usually alone, reveals his or her thoughts, emotions, and/or *motivations* without being heard by other characters. The convention was frequently employed during the Elizabethan era, and many of the best-known examples are from Shakespeare; for example, Hamlet's "To be, or not to be" speech is a soliloquy. Soliloquies differ from *dramatic monologues* in that dramatic monologues address an implied listener, while the speaker of a soliloquy thinks aloud or addresses the audience.

sonnet: a highly structured *lyric* poem, which normally has fourteen lines of *iambic pentameter*. We can distinguish four major variations of the sonnet.

Italian / Petrarchan: a sonnet type with an *octave* rhyming *abbaabba* and a *sestet* rhyming *cdecde* or *cdcdcd* (other arrangements are possible here). Usually, a turn in argument takes place between *octave* and *sestet*. The name "Petrarchan sonnet" refers to the Italian poet and humanist Francesco Petrarca, or Petrarch, who made extensive use of the form in his *Rime sparse* (*Scattered Rhymes*, c. 1327-74), an accomplished and highly influential collection of poems centered on the poet's unrequited love for a lady named Laura. See also *humanism / Renaissance humanism*.

Miltonic: developed by Milton (1608-74) and similar to the Petrarchan in rhyme scheme, but eliminating the turn after the octave, thus giving greater unity to the poem's structure of thought.

Shakespearean: often called the "English sonnet," this form has three *quatrains* and a *couplet*. The quatrains rhyme internally but do not interlock: *abab cdcd efef gg*. The turn may occur after the second quatrain, but is usually revealed in the final couplet. Shakespeare's sonnets are the best-known examples of this form.

Spenserian: after Edmund Spenser (c. 1552-99), who developed the form in his sonnet cycle *Amoretti*. This sonnet form has three quatrains linked through *interlocking rhyme*, and a separately rhyming couplet: *abab bcbc cdcd ee*.

Sophocles: see *anagnorisis, Hellenic / Hellenistic*.

speculative fiction: fiction that is typically suggestive of large ideas about human society, and that is set in a future or otherwise alternative world—but not necessarily fiction that focuses to any significant extent on science or technology. George Orwell's *Nineteen Eighty-Four* (1949) and Cormac McCarthy's *The Road* (2006), for example, may be classed as speculative fiction. *Star Trek* is clearly an example both of science fiction and of speculative fiction; an interesting question for discussion might be whether *Star Wars* is to any degree speculative fiction as well as science fiction.

Margaret Atwood (b. 1939) once rejected the notion that her novels *The Handmaid's Tale* and *Oryx and Crake* could properly be classed as science fiction, suggesting that they should instead be classed as speculative fiction. More recently she has acknowledged that the two categories are not mutually exclusive, and that it is not inappropriate to describe *The Handmaid's Tale* or *Oryx and Crake* as science fiction.

Spenser, Edmund: see *epic, epithalamion, prothalamion, sonnet (Spenserian), stanza.*

Spenserian sonnet: see *sonnet (Spenserian).*

Spenserian stanza: a nine-line stanza, with eight *iambic pentameters* and a concluding *alexandrine*, rhyming *ababbcbcc.*

Spiegelman, Art: see *graphic literature.*

Spinoza, Baruch: see *affect.*

Spivak, Gayatri: see *feminism / feminist criticism and theory / gender-based criticism and theory.*

spondee: a metrical *foot* containing two strongly stressed syllables: / / (e.g., "blind mouths").

Spooner, Rev. William: see *Spoonerism.*

Spoonerism: the accidental exchange of the beginning *phonemes* of two or more words. The phenomenon is named after Reverend William Spooner (1844-1930), famous for making such errors; for example, he is said to have toasted England's monarch as "the queer old dean." Spoonerisms are sometimes made intentionally as a form of humorous wordplay.

sprung rhythm: a modern variation of *accentual verse*, created by the English poet Gerard Manley Hopkins (1844-89), in which rhythms are determined largely by the number of strong stresses in a line, without regard to the number of unstressed syllables. Hopkins felt that sprung rhythm more closely approximated the natural rhythms of speech than did conventional poetry.

Stanton, Elizabeth Cady: see *parallelism*.

stanza: any lines of verse that are grouped together in a poem and separated from other similarly structured groups by a space. In metrical poetry, stanzas share metrical and rhyming patterns; however, stanzas may also be formed on the basis of thought, as in irregular odes. Conventional stanza forms include the *ballad stanza, ottava rima, quatrain, rhyme royal, Spenserian stanza,* and *tercet*.

steampunk: *fantasy* straddling the border with *science fiction*, drawing on elements from subcultures of the late twentieth and early twenty-first centuries but most strongly reflective of nineteenth-century aesthetics and technology—especially the technology of steam power, often powering retro-futuristic machines or devices. Steampunk fiction often takes place in the nineteenth century—but with reimagined technology—or in a post-apocalyptic future in which steam power has replaced twentieth- and twenty-first-century technologies.

Stein, Gertrude: see *language poetry*.

stichomythia: a pattern of dialogue in which two characters speak single metrical lines in a quickly alternating, usually tense exchange, sometimes involving repetition. Stichomythia is used frequently in classical drama, but is also occasionally employed by Elizabethan writers such as Shakespeare, as in this passage from *Hamlet*:

> QUEEN: Hamlet, thou hast thy father much offended.
> HAMLET: Mother, you have my father much offended.
> QUEEN: Come, come, you answer with an idle tongue.
> HAMLET: Go, go, you question with a wicked tongue.

stock character: a character defined by a set of characteristics that are stereotypical and/or established by literary convention; examples include the "wicked stepmother" and the "absent-minded professor."

Stoker, Bram: see *Gothic*.

Stoppard, Tom: see *absurdist*.

story: narrative material, independent of the manner in which it may be presented or the ways in which the narrative material may be organized. Story is thus distinct from *plot*.

Stowe, Harriet Beecher: see *apocryphal*.

stream of consciousness: a narrative technique that conveys the inner workings of a character's mind, in which a character's thoughts, feelings, memories, and impressions are related in an unbroken flow, without concern for *chronology* or coherence. The term appears to have first been used with reference to mental process by William James in his *Principles of Psychology* (1892). In the chapter he entitled "The Stream of Consciousness," James begins by observing that "within each personal consciousness states are always changing" and that "each personal consciousness is sensibly continuous." The term was applied to literature by May Sinclair in a 1918 review of Dorothy Richardson's groundbreaking 1915 novel *Pointed Roofs* (the first volume in what became the multi-volume *Pilgrimage* series)—though Richardson herself preferred to describe herself as employing *interior monologue* in her fiction.

The technique was perhaps most famously employed by Virginia Woolf (1882-1941) and James Joyce; Joyce's *Ulysses* (1922) concludes with a 44-page monologue from the point of view of the character Molly Bloom, which opens in this way:

> yes because he never did a thing like that before as ask to get his breakfast in bed with a couple of eggs since the *City Arms* hotel when he used to be pretending to be laid up with a sick voice doing his highness to make himself interesting to that old faggot Mrs Riordan that he thought he had a great leg of and she never left us a farthing all for masses for herself and her soul greatest miser ever was actually afraid to lay out 4d for her methylated spirit telling me all her ailments she had too much old chat in her about politics and earthquakes and the end of the world let us have a bit of fun first ...

Some critics apply the term "stream of consciousness" only to passages such as this one, which are written entirely in the first person. The term is also often used more loosely, though, to refer to any one of (or combination of) a range of techniques that attempt to convey in prose fiction a sense of the progression of thoughts and sensations occurring within a character's mind; extended passages of prose fiction written in *free indirect discourse*, for example, are often described as employing a stream of consciousness technique.

stress: see *accent*.

Strindberg, August: see *expressionism / impressionism*.

strophe: the first stanza in a Pindaric *ode*. This is followed by an *antistrophe*, which presents the same metrical pattern and rhyme scheme, and finally by an *epode*, differing in *meter* from the preceding stanzas. Upon completion of this "triad," the entire sequence can recur. "Strophe" may also describe a stanza or other subdivision in other kinds of poem.

structuralism / poststructuralism: Structuralism is a theoretical approach based on the argument that all meaning in a culture depends upon and is produced by underlying systems of rules. These rules are not based upon any reality beyond culture; instead, they derive their importance from their relationships to the other rules within the system. Structuralism focuses on these systems of rules, rather than on the actions of individual people, as producers of meaning.

Structuralism was popularized through the work of the linguist Ferdinand de Saussure (1857-1913), who argued that the relationship between a particular concept (the "signified") and the word or other expression which refers to that concept (the "signifier") is wholly arbitrary. Each combination of signified and signifier—which Saussure called a "sign"—therefore possesses meaning only through its specific position in a larger system of signs. Saussure also drew a distinction between "langue"—the system of language, including grammatical conventions and the definitions of words—and "parole," actual instances of speech or writing. (See *semiotics*.)

In the 1950s, important thinkers from outside linguistics began to take structuralist approaches, adapting Saussure's major insights to their own disciplines, including Claude Lévi-

Strauss (1908-2009) in anthropology, Jacques Lacan (1901-81) in psychoanalysis, and Roland Barthes (1915-80) in literary and cultural studies. Saussure's distinction between "langue" and "parole" became the model for a more general distinction between systems of conventions and specific instances in which those conventions were enacted, with structuralist thinkers focusing on the underlying structures instead of on individuals or individual events or behaviors. In the context of literary studies, for example, structuralist analysis tends to show less interest in the artistic importance of specific literary works and more interest in the systems of rules that operate to produce meaning within and across works of literature.

Structuralist thinkers of the mid-twentieth century also expanded on Saussure's claim that the relationship between a signifier and its signified was arbitrary, arguing that all sorts of cultural meanings that might seem natural or essential were in fact the products of an underlying system; they applied this type of analysis to everything from gender roles and the concept of individual personality to clothing fashions and the choice to drink wine instead of beer.

The term "poststructuralist" is applied to theories that build on some aspects of structuralism while rejecting others; generally, poststructuralists accept structuralism's basic tenet that all meaning in cultures is produced by systems of rules (such as the system of linguistic signs), but they argue that such systems are inherently unstable and continually changing, and that therefore all the meanings, truths, and forms of knowledge such systems produce are also unstable and impermanent.

Jacques Derrida (1930-2004), one of the theorists most strongly associated with poststructuralism, argued that if all meaning comes from structures such as language, it is impossible for theorists ever to see outside them—meaning that all

S

theorizing about structures is limited because it depends on a position within a structure. He also argued that if, as Saussure claimed, signs derive their meaning from their relationships to other signs, this means that language is profoundly unstable: it has no ultimate foundation, and any word, supposedly defined in opposition to other words, carries traces of the meanings of those other words. *Deconstruction* is an approach aimed at highlighting and dissecting these instabilities.

Another theorist linked to poststructuralism is Michel Foucault (1926-84), who argued that power enforces and polices systems of linguistic and cultural meanings (called "discourses") by foreclosing some forms of knowledge and privileging others. Foucault was particularly interested in the ways in which power produces individual identities and senses of selfhood.

style: a distinctive or specific use of language and form.

sublime: a concept, most prominent during the *Romantic* era, of the qualities of grandeur, power, and awe that may be inherent in or produced by undomesticated nature or great art. The sublime was thought of as higher and more profound than the merely beautiful.

subplot: a line of story that is subordinate to the main storyline of a narrative. (Note that properly speaking a subplot is a category of *story* material, not of *plot*.)

substitution: a deliberate change from the dominant pattern of stresses in a line of verse to create emphasis or variation. Thus the first line of Shakespeare's sonnet "Shall I compare thee to a summer's day?" is decidedly *iambic* in *meter* (x / x / x / x / x /), whereas the second line substitutes a *trochee* (/ x) in the opening *foot*: "Thou art more lovely and more temperate."

subtext: implied or suggested meaning of a passage of text, or of an entire work.

surrealism: one of the many influential schools within *modernism*. Like *realism*, surrealism incorporates elements of the true appearance of life and nature; but unlike realism, it combines these elements according to a logic more typical of dreams than of waking life. Isolated aspects of surrealist art may create powerful illusions of reality, but the effect of the whole is usually to disturb or question our sense of reality rather than to confirm it.

Surrey, Henry Howard, Earl of: see *blank verse*.

syllabic verse: poetry in which the length of a line is measured solely by the number of syllables, regardless of accents or patterns of stress.

syllable: vocal sound or group of sounds forming a unit of speech; a syllable may be formed with a single effort of articulation. Some syllables consist of a single *phoneme* (e.g., the word "I," or the first syllable in the word "u-ni-ty") but others may be made up of several phonemes (as with one-syllable words such as "lengths," "splurged," and "through"). By contrast, the much shorter words "ago," "any," and "open" each have two syllables.

symbol: a word, image, or idea that represents itself, but also goes beyond this in suggesting other meanings. Like *metaphor*, the symbol extends meaning; but while the tenor and vehicle of metaphor are bound in a specific relationship, a symbol may have a range of connotations. For example, the image of a rose may call forth associations of love, passion, transience, fragility, youth, and beauty, among others. Depending upon the context, such an image could be interpreted in a variety of ways; the "roses and white lilies" in Thomas Campion's "There Is a Garden in Her

Face" (1617) suggest a different set of meanings than the rose in Blake's lyric "The Sick Rose" (1794).

symbolist movement: a late-nineteenth-century French movement of writers who rejected *realism* and associated attempts to depict objective reality, instead attempting to express emotions, interior thoughts, spiritual realizations, and abstract ideas through metaphor. Rather than describing their subject matter directly, symbolists strove to suggest insights and emotional states through evocative symbols, sound, and sense imagery. Important Symbolist authors include Stéphane Mallarmé (1842-98), Paul Verlaine (1844-96), and Arthur Rimbaud (1854-91). The movement played an influential role in the development of *modernism*.

synaesthesia: in psychology, the facility of forming strong associative connections between one sense and another; such associations may be, for example, between different colors and different numbers or letters of the alphabet, or between different colors or shapes and different words or musical sounds. Someone with synaesthesia might involuntarily "see" the letter L as green, for example, or the number 6 as blue. In literature, the term refers to a type of *metaphor* in which a sensory experience is described in the language of a different sense, such as the description of a sound in terms of color (e.g., "a dark voice") or of taste in terms of touch (e.g., "cold smell" in Seamus Heaney's 1966 poem "Digging").

syncope: in poetry, the dropping of a letter or syllable from the middle of a word, as in "trav'ler." Such a contraction allows a line to stay within a metrical scheme. See also *catalexis* and *elision*.

synecdoche: a kind of *metonymy* in which a writer substitutes the name of a part of something to signify the whole: for example, "sail" for ship or "hand" for a member of the ship's crew.

Synge, J.M.: see *Irish Literary Renaissance*.

syntax: sentence structure; i.e., the order of words within sentences, or the rules governing the grammatically correct arrangement of words. Syntax is an important element of expressive *style*.

tail-rhyme: a verse form employing six- or twelve-line stanzas made up of long couplets alternating with short individual lines. All the short lines in a given stanza rhyme with each other, while the couplets may rhyme individually or with each other, such that the rhyme scheme of a six-line stanza, for example, could be *aabaab* or *aabccb*. The form was most commonly used during the medieval period, especially in verse *romance*, but has also been employed by more recent poets; the following example is from Thomas Gray's "Ode on the Death of a Favorite Cat, Drowned in a Tub of Gold Fishes" (1748):

> From hence, ye beauties, undeceived,
> Know, one false step is ne'er retrieved,
>   And be with caution bold.
> Not all that tempts your wand'ring eyes
> And heedless hearts is lawful prize;
>   Nor all that glisters gold.

Tate, Allen: see *New Criticism*.

Tennyson, Lord Alfred: see *dramatic monologue / persona poem / dramatic poem, elegy, In Memoriam poem, monodrama*.

tenor: see *metaphor*.

tercet: a group, or stanza, of three lines, often linked by an *interlocking rhyme* scheme as in *terza rima*. See also *triplet*.

terza rima: an arrangement of *tercets* interlocked by a rhyme scheme of *aba bcb cdc ded*, etc., and ending with a couplet that rhymes with the second-last line of the final tercet (for example, *efe ff*). One well-known example is Percy Shelley's "Ode to the West Wind" (1819).

tetralogy: a set of four novels, films, plays, or other works that are distinct but linked, usually by thematic or narrative elements.

tetrameter: a line of poetry containing four metrical *feet*.

textual criticism: the scholarly analysis of the surviving versions of a pre-existing written work and any related documents.

theater-in-the-round: a type of staging in which seating for the audience surrounds the stage on all (or at least most) of its sides. This approach was common in ancient Greek, ancient Roman, and medieval theater; it was not often used after the seventeenth century, but in the mid-twentieth century its popularity increased, especially in experimental theater. Also called "arena theater."

theme: in general, an idea explored in a work through character, action, and/or image. To be fully developed, however, a theme must consist of more than a single concept or idea: it should also include an argument about the idea. Thus if a poem examines the topic of jealousy, we might say the theme is that jealousy undermines love or that jealousy is a manifestation of insecurity. Few, if any, literary works have single themes.

Theory: a shorthand term that came into currency in the late twentieth century. It is generally used to refer to a diverse body of concepts and modes of thought that position themselves to a greater or lesser degree as being in opposition to traditional approaches in the humanities. The diverse body of approaches that is brought together in this way is to some extent also loosely connected in sharing a tendency to call into question presumed links between the worlds of words and ideas and the "real" world. Those opposed to what they call Theory also sometimes use the term pejoratively with reference to what they perceive to be shared styles of discourse that are unnecessarily dense or opaque.

Theory draws on a wide range of disciplines, from history and philosophy to economics and linguistics. In the context of literary studies, a growing tendency to apply these approaches to the reading of literature and other cultural products has provoked a great deal of controversy, especially in the late 1970s and 1980s. *Russian formalism*, some forms of *psychoanalytic criticism*, *deconstruction*, *structuralism*, *poststructuralism*, and *semiotics* may all be included under the umbrella of Theory.

Several sorts of theoretical work, it should be noted, are not generally classed as part of Theory with a capital T: theories from earlier eras; theories that tend not to challenge received notions in the ways that Theory challenges them; and theories that tend to affirm rather than call into question possibilities for words and ideas connecting more or less reliably to a "real" world. Aristotle's theory of tragedy, Darwin's theory of natural selection, Northrop Frye's *Anatomy of Criticism* (1957), Erich Auerbach's *Mimesis* (1946), and A.D. Nuttall's *A New Mimesis* (1983) are all examples of theoretical work that would not be considered part of Theory.

third-person narrative: see *narrative perspective*.

Thomas, Dylan: see *rhyme (interlocking rhyme)*, *villanelle*.

Thomson, James: see *georgic*.

Thoreau, Henry David: see *Transcendentalism*.

Tolkien, J.R.R.: see *fantasy*, *mythopoeic theory and criticism*.

Tolstoy, Leo: see *intrusive narrator*.

Tomkins, Silvan: see *affect*.

tone: in a work of literature, the attitude toward a given subject or audience, as expressed though an authorial persona or "voice." Tone can be projected through particular choices of wording, *imagery*, *figures of speech*, and rhythmic devices. Compare *mood*.

Toomer, Jean: see *Harlem Renaissance*.

tragedy: in the traditional definition originating in discussions of ancient Greek drama, a serious narrative recounting the downfall of the protagonist. More loosely, the term has been applied to a wide variety of literary forms in which the tone is predominantly a dark one and the narrative does not end happily. For Aristotelian concepts relating to tragedy, see *anagnorisis*, *catharsis*, *hamartia*, and *peripeteia*.

tragi-comedy: a genre of drama in which many elements of *tragedy* are present, but which generally has a happy ending.

Transcendentalism: a body of philosophical, religious, social, and literary thought that flourished in New England in the 1830s and 1840s; its major figures include Ralph Waldo Emerson (1803-82) and Henry David Thoreau (1817-62). Strongly influenced by English *Romanticism*, Transcendentalists believed in the importance of individual intuition and saw both human beings and nature as innately divine; they also tended to oppose religious dogmatism and advocate social reform. The Transcendentalists themselves primarily wrote poetry and non-fiction prose, and their ideas significantly impacted American literature, including the work of such writers as Walt Whitman (1819-92) and Herman Melville (1819-91).

Tremblay, Michel: see *chorus*.

trilogy: a set of three novels, films, plays, or other works that are distinct but linked, usually by theme or narrative elements.

trimeter: a line of poetry containing three metrical *feet*.

triolet: a French form of eight lines in which the first and second lines appear multiple times. The first line is repeated at lines 4 and 7; the second line is repeated at line 8. The triolet has only two rhymes: *abaaabab*.

triple foot: a poetic *foot* of three syllables. The possible varieties of triple foot are the *anapest* (in which two unstressed syllables are followed by a stressed syllable), the *dactyl* (in which a stressed syllable is followed by two unstressed syllables), and the *molossus* (in which all three syllables are stressed equally). English poetry tends to use *duple* rhythms far more frequently than triple rhythms.

triple rhyme: see *rhyme*.

triplet: a group of three lines with the same end-rhyme, much used by eighteenth-century poets to vary or punctuate the flow of *couplets*. See also *tercet*.

trochee: a metrical *foot* containing one strong stress followed by one weak stress: / x (e.g., "heaven," "lover").

trope: any figure of speech that plays on our understandings of words to extend, alter, or transform "literal" meaning. Common tropes include *hyperbole*, *metaphor*, *metonymy*, *oxymoron*, *personification*, *simile*, and *synecdoche*. See also *figures of speech*.

troubadours: twelfth- to mid-fourteenth-century poets who entertained (and, in some cases, were themselves members of) the noble class of southern France. Their lyrics, written for musical performance and often centered on the subject of idealized love, influenced literature across Western Europe.

t

true rhyme: see *rhyme*.

turn: (Italian "volta") the point in a *sonnet* where the mood or argument changes. The turn may occur between the *octave* and *sestet*, i.e., after the eighth line, or in the final *couplet*, depending on the kind of sonnet.

Twain, Mark: see *picaresque narrative*.

uncanny, the: from the German term *das Unheimliche*, the literal meaning of which is the opposite of "what is familiar." The uncanny is an unsettling feeling of eeriness most famously explored by Sigmund Freud in his 1919 essay "The Uncanny." According to Freud, the sensation of the uncanny is produced when repressed concepts are brought to mind or when psychologically significant boundaries are transgressed, such as the distinction between the familiar and the unfamiliar or the divide between the real and the imaginary. Although certain elements— such as ghosts, doubled characters, or robots with human qualities—are more likely to evoke the uncanny, in fiction their effect depends on context; for example, magic is rarely uncanny in the context of a fairytale, but it may be so in the context of an otherwise realistic story.

unexpurgated: appearing in complete form, without material censored for sexual or otherwise controversial content.

unities: many literary theorists of the late sixteenth through late eighteenth centuries held that a play should ideally be presented as representing a single place, and confining the action to a single day and a single dominant event. They disapproved of plots involving gaps or long periods of time, shifts in place, or subplots. These concepts, which came to be referred to as the unities of space, time, and action, were based on a misreading of classical authorities (principally of Aristotle).

unreliable narrator: see *narrative perspective.*

unstressed rhyme: see *rhyme.*

Ur-text: German word meaning "original text"; in cases where a presumed original version is lost, an Ur-text is one reconstructed based on an examination of the available later versions.

Utopian literature: literature depicting an imagined perfect state or society. Thomas More first used the word in his 1516 work *Utopia*—a pun on the Greek words for "no place" and "good place"—but invented ideal societies have existed in literature at least since Plato's *Republic* (c. 400 BCE). A related concept is "dystopia," an imagined undesirable society, often one that warns against problems in the real world by exaggerating them.

van Dijk, Teun A.: see *discourse analysis.*

Van Gogh, Vincent: see *expressionism / impressionism.*

vehicle: see *metaphor.*

Verfremdungseffekt: see *alienation effect.*

verisimilitude: the appearance of truth, or, in a literary context, illusion of believability. The term is most often used to describe *realistic* works, but it can also be applied to works that incorporate improbable or impossible elements, as long as they seem credible within the context of the work.

Verlaine, Paul: see *symbolist movement.*

vernacular: broadly understood, vernacular speech is informal, everyday speech. More precisely, "vernacular" refers to the native language or non-standard dialect of an area—especially when an elite group in that area speaks a different language or dialect.

Verne, Jules: see *science fiction*.

***vers de société*:** French: literally, "verse about society." The term originated with poetry written by aristocrats and upper-middle-class poets that specifically disavows the ambition of creating "high art" while treating the concerns of their own group in verse forms that demonstrate a high degree of formal control (e.g., artful rhymes, surprising turns of diction).

vers libre (French): see *free verse*.

verse: a general term for works of poetry, usually referring to poems that incorporate some kind of metrical structure. The term may also describe a line of poetry, though more frequently it is applied to a stanza.

verse form: the configuration of metrical lines in a poem. This can include patterns of rhyme, repetition of stanzas, or conformity to a pre-existing *fixed form*, but none of these elements is necessary; several lines of unrhymed blank verse constitutes a verse form as much as does a *sonnet* or a *haiku*.

verso: the back side of a page—or, in a bound book, the left-side pages; the opposite is *recto*, which refers to the front sides of loose pages or the right-side pages in a book.

Vice: in medieval drama, a despicable, often comically entertaining character who tempts the hero toward evil.

villanelle: a poem usually consisting of 19 lines, with five three-line stanzas (*tercets*) rhyming *aba*, and a concluding *quatrain* rhyming *abaa*. The first and third lines of the first tercet are repeated at fixed intervals throughout the rest of the poem. A well-known example is Dylan Thomas's "Do Not Go Gentle into That Good Night" (1951).

Virgil: see *blank verse, georgic, humanism / Renaissance humanism.*

voice: As a grammatical term, voice is quite precise: when the subject of a verb is performing the action, the verb is in the active voice (e.g., "he prepared dinner"), whereas when the subject is having the action done to him/her/it/them, the verb is in the passive voice (e.g., "dinner was prepared").

When people speak of the voice of a particular writer, though—or the voice of a particular character—they are referring to the expressive style of that individual writer or character. Voice in this latter sense is a matter of *tone,* of *diction* and *syntax*—of personality as expressed through writing style.

volta: see *turn.*

Vorticism: *avant-garde modernist* movement that flourished in London in 1913-15 under the leadership of Wyndham Lewis; although it was primarily a visual art movement, its principles were also extended to literature, notably by Ezra Pound (1885-1972). Strongly influenced by *futurism,* Vorticism's abstract, aggressive aesthetic drew on technology and industry and was intended to achieve the greatest possible intensity and dynamic energy.

Walker, Alice: see *epistolary novel.*

Waller, Fats: see *Harlem Renaissance.*

Walpole, Horace: see *Gothic.*

Warner, Michael: see *queer theory.*

Warren, Robert Penn: see *roman à clef.*

Watt, Ian: see *delayed decoding.*

weak rhyme: see *rhyme.*

W

Webster, Augusta: see *dramatic monologue / persona poem / dramatic poem*.

well-made play: a play with a plot structured in order to produce building suspense, a climax, and a resolution that is part of an ordered conclusion. This approach, developed in nineteenth-century France under the name *pièce bien faite*, has been extremely influential, but "well-made play" soon became a pejorative term for plays with effective mechanisms of plot but superficial content.

Wells, H.G.: see *animal studies, science fiction*.

Whitman, Walt: see *epistrophe / epiphora, Transcendentalism*.

Wilde, Oscar: see *Irish Literary Renaissance*.

Williams, Raymond: see *cultural materialism / cultural studies, Marxist theory and criticism, print culture / history of the book*.

Wimsatt, W.K.: see *intentional fallacy, New Criticism*.

wit: The concept of "wit" has a range of related meanings and has been interpreted with a different emphasis in each historical period. Initially understood broadly to mean intelligence or knowledge, in the sixteenth century wit took on a connotation of inventiveness in literary expression; by the eighteenth century, it was understood to suggest the elegant articulation of astute perceptions. During the era of *Romanticism*, the status of wit decreased and its definition began to narrow to the understanding of wit most common today: verbal cleverness or adept, often ironic, joking.

Wolfe, Cary: see *animal studies*.

Woolf, Virginia: see *feminism / feminist criticism and theory / gender-based criticism and theory, modernism, novel, stream of consciousness.*

Wordsworth, William: see *Neo-Platonism, ode.*

Wyatt, Sir Thomas: see *humanism / Renaissance humanism.*

Wycherley, William: see *comedy of manners, Restoration comedy.*

Yeats, W.B.: see *Irish Literary Renaissance, ottava rima.*

Zeitgeist: a German word usually translated as "spirit of the age"; it refers to an era's dominant mood or cultural character, which is reflected in the historical events and cultural products of that era.

zeugma: a *figure of speech* (*trope*) in which one word links or "yokes" two others in the same sentence, often to comic or ironic effect. For example, a verb may govern two objects, as in Alexander Pope's line "Or stain her honour, or her new brocade."

from the publisher

A name never says it all, but the word "broadview" expresses a good deal of the philosophy behind our company. We are open to a broad range of academic approaches and political viewpoints. We pay attention to the broad impact book publishing and book printing has in the wider world; we began using recycled stock more than a decade ago, and for some years now we have used 100% recycled paper for most titles. As a Canadian-based company we naturally publish a number of titles with a Canadian emphasis, but our publishing program overall is internationally oriented and broad-ranging. Our individual titles often appeal to a broad readership too; many are of interest as much to general readers as to academics and students.

Founded in 1985, Broadview remains a fully independent company owned by its shareholders—not an imprint or subsidiary of a larger multinational.

If you would like to find out more about Broadview and about the books we publish, please visit us at **www.broadviewpress.com**. And if you'd like to place an order through the site, we'd like to show our appreciation by extending a special discount to you: by entering the code below you will receive a 20% discount on purchases made through the Broadview website.

Discount code: **broadview20%**

Thank you for choosing Broadview.

Please note: this offer applies only to sales of bound books within the United States or Canada.

The interior of this book is printed on 100% recycled paper.